An Inside Look at Your Favorite Writers

Published by
Beyond Words Publishing, Inc.
20827 NW Cornell Road, Suite 500
Hillsboro, Oregon 97124
503-531-8700/1-800-284-9673

Cover & Interior Design: Big-Giant Inc.

Publicity photos reprinted with kind permission from the following:

Andrew Clements by Bill Crofton, courtesy of Simon & Schuster Children's
Publishing Division; Avi by Lorie K. Stover, courtesy of Houghton Mifflin Company;
J.K. Rowling by Scott Olson; J.K. Rowling cover photo by Janis Campbell; Lois
Lowry cover photo courtesy of Houghton Mifflin Company; Lois Lowry interior photo
© Margret Lowry, reprinted with the permission by Houghton Mifflin Company;
Brian Jacques by David Jacques, courtesy of Penquin Putnam Books for Young
Readers; Louis Sachar courtesy of Random House Children's Books; Jack Gantos by
Merry Scully courtesy of Farrar, Straus & Giroux; Patricia Polacco by Kenn Klein,
courtesy of Philomel Books; Christopher Paul Curtis by James Keyser, courtesy of
Random House Children's Books; Paula Danziger by Sigrid Estrada, courtesy of
Penguin Putnam Books for Young Readers; Margare Peterson Haddix courtesy of
Simon & Schuster Children's Publishing Division.

ISBN: 1-58270-073-7

Printed in the United States of America
Distributed to the book trade by Publishers Group West

Library of Congress Cataloging-in-Publication Data

Campbell, Janis (Janis M.)
    Authors by request : an inside look at your favorite writers / written by Janis
Campbell and Catherine Collison.
    p. cm.
    Summary: A collection of interviews in which authors, including J. K. Rowling,
Brian Jacques, and R. L. Stine, share writing tips, reading lists and personal stories
about their work.
    ISBN 1-58270-073-7 (pbk.)
    1. Children's literature, American—History and criticism—Juvenile literature.
2. Children's literature, English—History and criticism—Juvenile literature.
3. Authors, American—20th century—Biography—Juvenile literature. 4. Authors,
English—20th century—Biography—Juvenile literature. 5. Creative writing—
Juvenile literature. [1. American literature—History and criticism. 2. English literature—History and criticism. 3. Authors, American. 4. Authors, English.
5. Authorship. 6. Creative writing.] I. Collison, Catherine. II. Title.

PS490 .C36 2002
810.9'9282—dc21
2001058953

The corporate mission of Beyond Words Publishing, Inc:
Inspire to Integrity

An Inside Look at Your Favorite Writers

Janis Campbell & Cathy Collison

Publishing

Acknowledgments

Thanks to all of the authors who generously answered our many questions. We interviewed each of the authors included in this book at least twice, some many times, either in person or by phone or email. Thanks as well to the various publishing houses and publicity staffs for their help in contacting the authors and answering our final questions, as well as providing photos for the book.

Thanks especially to Beyond Words for publishing this book and for sharing our enthusiasm about great books for young readers. We would also like to thank our husbands, Steve Campbell and Bill Collison, who were the first readers of *Authors by Request*. And a special thanks to Bill for late-night copy editing and good advice!

Note: The authors plan to use a portion of any royalties earned by this book to purchase and donate books to nonprofit organizations dedicated to promoting children's literacy.

Table of Contents

Introduction

*H*ave you ever wanted to know the stories of the people behind today's most requested books?

We did, too. So we found out. And the stories are amazing! Did you know that R. L. Stine used to write little joke books and pass them out to friends at school? (His teacher didn't find them funny and took them away.) Or that J. K. Rowling started her writing career when she was six? (Her first story was about a rabbit.)

These are just some of the fun facts you will learn in this book about your favorite authors. Want to know what they were like when they were growing up, or how they became writers? Then read on. In school, some were shy, some were class clowns, and some became teachers. Some overcame learning disabilities. Others worked in a variety of jobs to make a living before they became full-time writers. Can you guess who worked in an auto factory? At a newspaper? On a shipping dock?

You have probably heard of all the writers we have profiled in this book: Brian Jacques, Paula Danziger, J. K. Rowling, Jack Gantos, Christopher Paul Curtis, Louis Sachar, Patricia Polacco, R. L. Stine, Lois Lowry, Andrew Clements, Margaret Peterson Haddix, and Avi. If any of these names are new to you though, be sure to check out their books after you read their real-life stories.

Who are we? We are newspaper journalists who write and edit stories for young readers. We've interviewed many authors over the years for *Yak's Corner*, a magazine for young readers published by the Detroit Free Press, and a nationally syndicated newspaper feature. We've also been reviewing books for many years. When we were given the opportunity to write this book for Beyond Words, we had to make a tough decision—picking a dozen favorites from a long list of great writers for young people.

Where did we start? With our favorite books. As book reviewers, it's our job to keep up on the latest books for young readers. We read dozens of books every month so we can help kids find great things to read. This book features twelve very different writers who represent the very best in books for young people. They write in a variety of styles, but all of them create stellar stories that are memorable, magical, and destined to be on bookshelves for many years to come. In working on this book, we were inspired by the stories they shared with us. We think that you will be, too.

Authors by Request also offers you practical advice and cool tips to try in your own writing. Who knows? Someday your books may be requested as often as those of the authors profiled here. Maybe we'll be asking you to tell us *your* life story!

Brian Jacques

Adventures Big Enough
for . . . a Mouse?

*B*rian Jacques's first animal story got him into a heap of trouble. When the creator of the famous animal adventure series Redwall was just ten, he wrote a story about a bird cleaning a crocodile's teeth. The story was so good, his teacher didn't believe Brian had written it himself. "He was a nasty little swine," says Brian of that teacher.

Brian Jacques (pronounced JAKES) remembers that teacher as being particularly mean. He carried a cane. And if a student couldn't answer one of his questions, "he'd whack you."

"He told us to write something about the peculiarities of animals," says Brian. Brian remembers reading a *Ripley's Believe It or Not* column about unusual things and weird facts, which ran in the Sunday newspaper. Brian used the column as a basis for his fictional essay about the bird and the crocodile.

"I wrote a whole essay about it. My teacher said, 'Where did you copy this?' I said I didn't copy it. He said, 'How old are you?' I said, 'Ten.' He said, 'Boys of ten can't write like this. Now, where did you copy it?'"

Brian stuck to his story, which was true. His teacher scolded him, saying, "A liar is worse than a thief."

Brian had the bad luck of having that teacher for two years!

But he also had some good teachers along the way. His favorite, just before he left school, was Mr. Thomas.

Mr. Thomas was popular with all the boys at school. He was "a big, hulking man" who had been captain of a commando unit during World War II. He told the boys tons of exciting war stories.

Outside of school, Brian didn't spend much time writing. He was too busy working.

Personal Stuff

Born: June 15, 1939, in Liverpool, England

Family: Brian has two grown sons and one dog, Teddy, a West Highland Terrier. He lives in Liverpool.

Free time: Brian loves doing crossword puzzles, cooking dinners for family gatherings, and having parties with plenty of music and friends. He loves singing folk music and opera, spending time with his grand-daughter, Hannah, and taking Teddy for walks.

Favorite books: In his teens, Brian enjoyed poetry and Greek myths. Today, he reads western writer Larry McMurtry, British humorist P. G. Wodehouse, and popular American fiction writer Mario Puzo.

Past jobs: Delivery boy, merchant seaman, dock worker, milk truck driver, bus driver, railway worker, standup comic, writer for a local theater, and newspaper columnist. Brian still does a Sunday radio show in Liverpool.

When he was nine, he got his first job as a delivery boy for a grocery store in his neighborhood in Liverpool, England. Later on, he worked delivering carpet. "I was a big, strong lad. I could carry a roll of flooring on my shoulder."

Although Brian wasn't encouraged as a writer in school, he knew he was very good at it. "I was the best in my class," he says, and he wasn't afraid to admit it.

Still, Brian never thought his writing was the stuff of a career. In his working-class neighborhood, most boys dreamed of going to sea.

And that's what Brian did. At fifteen, he finished school, joined a boat crew, and went to sea as a merchant marine. He sailed all over the world.

"But I soon became disenchanted with that," he says. "When I came back, I went to work on the docks."

Working on the docks was a great job in Liverpool at the time. Brian had many other jobs—he worked on the railway, on building sites—but he always came back to the docks where he knew he could find good work.

By the time Brian was in his late thirties, he was driving a milk truck. (Yes, they really used to deliver fresh milk right to your door every morning—just like the newspaper!)

One of Brian's favorite stops on his milk route was a school for the blind in Liverpool. Brian would help bring in the milk, and then one of the housemothers would feed him sandwiches and tea.

Brian quit delivering milk to move on to more exciting jobs. He began working as a stand-up comic, and he wrote

Try This

Brian gets loads of fan mail, and many young writers share their own stories. One fan wrote and told him he was writing a book called "Greenwall." Brian told him, "You must learn to write originally. You must learn to paint your own picture."

Brian advises young writers to "learn to trust their imagination. Make yourself relax, shake free of all the things you worry about everyday, and let your imagination run wild. The second thing is, learn to paint pictures with words. It's really very simple. You write what you see and feel in your imagination, and you learn to write it as vividly as you see it in your mind . . . painting pictures with words. There is a difference between writing 'There is a big tree in the woods,' and 'In the forest stood a great and ancient oak, heavy with history, whose canopy blotched out the sky and filtered sunlight to the ground below.'"

If you admire Brian's writing, try creating your own cool imaginary place. Even though Brian writes about animals, many of his character ideas come from his own adventures, including his days at sea. Right now, your main experience is your school life—so why not create an imaginary school? You pick the time period—maybe it's far off in the future, or way back in the past. Start painting your picture.

plays and one-act shows for a local theater. Eventually, he landed a job as a host on a radio show.

One Christmas, several years later, he was asked to help the radio station by attending a special school fair. He got to the event and realized it was for the blind students at the same school he had once delivered milk to.

"Oh, I know this lot, I used to deliver their milk," says Brian. "I got chatting to the headmaster, who said the school was in a bit of a fix financially."

So Brian helped out. He invited the children of the school to sing Christmas songs on his radio program. The publicity helped raise money for the school and renewed Brian's friendship with the students and teachers. Brian soon began visiting the school to read and spend time with the kids. (Brian continues to support the school today, both privately and through his radio show.)

But he found the reading a bit boring and didn't like most of the stories he read. "Too modern," he says. He loved adventure stories. As a kid, he especially loved the British classics like *Treasure Island*, by Robert Louis Stevenson.

And that's how *Redwall* got started.

Wise Words

" I am asked all the time whether I can give young writers any tips on writing. I deeply believe that if you're meant to be a writer, you will be a writer and no power on earth will be able to stop you from writing; it's a compulsion, like eating or breathing. I have written all my life, from the time I was a small child until the present. The difference being that I didn't know I would ever be a published author, let alone a successful one. "

Book List

Redwall (1986), **Mossflower** (1988), **Mattimeo** (1989), **Mariel of Redwall** (1991), **Salamandastron** (1992), **Martin the Warrior** (1993), **The Bellmaker** (1994), **Outcast of Redwall** (1995), **The Great Redwall Feast** (1996; a Redwall picture book), **The Pearls of Lutra** (1996), **The Long Patrol** (1997), **Marlfox** (1997), **The Legend of Luke** (1999), **Lord Brocktree** (2001), **Taggerung** (2001), **A Redwall Winter's Tale** (2001; a Redwall picture book)

Brian wanted to write a better story for kids at the school.

He spent seven months writing the first Redwall book by hand. The story is filled with mice, rats, and other woodland critters that live in the make-believe medieval world of Redwall Abbey. Brian's books are rich with detail, from the descriptions of the characters to what's on the menu.

Readers get to read about a huge feast preparation early in the first book. The "grayling a la Redwall" is a fantastic fish seasoned with "white gooseberry wine, rosemary, thyme, beech-nuts, and honey." Other courses include "tender freshwater shrimp garnished with cream and rose leaves, devilled barley pearls in acorn puree, apple and carrot chews, marinated cabbage stalks steeped in creamed white turnip with nutmeg." For critter food, it sure sounds good!

One thing is clear from reading Brian's work: he loves to cook and loves to eat. Brian says he cooks for his family once a week. His aim is "to make sure I get to see my boys from time to time. They are grown men with lives of their own, and although they live in Liverpool, it sometimes becomes difficult with their schedules and my schedule to get together. So the once-a-week family dinner serves that purpose well."

But there's another story behind the mouth-watering menus of Redwall Abbey. "The fabulous feasts I try to create for Redwall come from an entirely different history," Brian says. "When I was a lad growing up in Liverpool, we were extremely poor. Sometimes there were two or three days when we had nothing to eat . . . and I mean nothing! And you must remember this was during World War II, when the German Luftwaffe was bombing us daily. No one had food.

"My aunt, who lived just down the road, had these wonderful old cookbooks. I used to sit and look at the pictures of pies and cakes, and tarts, and great, huge hams, and salads . . . wonderful pictures they were!"

Brian says the cookbooks made his mouth water with their descriptions. But he never found any good food in the fictional books he read. "It used to drive me completely bonkers when I

AMAZING...

Unlike nearly every writer, Brian doesn't do much rewriting. He's one of the very lucky people whose stories are worked and reworked in his head before he ever puts them on paper, writing them out longhand instead of on a computer. This is even more amazing considering how rich with characters and details Brian's books are!

But True!

would read in some story or book 'and the King gave a great feast for all his people.' And I would think, 'Hang on now! What did the King serve? Was there enough for everybody? What did they eat? What did they drink? And just what is "mead" anyway? Were there tons of pastries for everyone? Was there music and singing? Did they all have a great

Where Write

You can write to Brian at this address:

**Redwall Readers Club
P.O. Box 57
Mossley Hill
L18 3NZ
U.K.**

Read more about Brian Jacques at:

www.redwall.org.

time?' So when I wrote my stories, I made sure that I described, in minute detail, the feasts at Redwall Abbey."

Of course, the Redwall books are filled with stories of more than just feasts. The stories take place in a world of animals and involve Good battling Evil. Just as the feasts seem so real, so do the many characters and places in these amazing adventures.

Brian was forty-six when the first book was published. "I just sat down and began writing. Sometimes I wrote all night."

He did his writing late at night after a full day's work. "I was ducking and dodging to make ends meet," he says. He had two young sons and a wife to support.

"The sun would be up and my sons would be getting ready for school, and they'd say, 'What are you writing, Dad?' I'd say, 'You just get yourself ready for school.'"

The whole story came out to be 800 pages—written on recycled paper.

He loaded the huge pile of pages into a shopping bag and was on his way to the school for the blind, to share them with the students. He stopped by the theater (where he also worked as a writer) and ran into the chairman, Alan Durband. They had a cup of coffee and talked about what they'd been doing.

Brian thought his friend's time was too valuable to bother him with reading his new children's story. Alan insisted. "If you've written it, I'll read it."

So Brian let him read it.

Alan loved *Redwall*. He told Brian he had finally figured out what Brian was meant to be—a writer for children. He sent Brian's manuscript to a publisher.

A few months later, the publisher asked Brian to sign a contract to write five books, which we now know as the Redwall series. Finally, he could settle down and focus on what he was always meant to do, from the time he was ten: be a writer of fabulous animal tales.

How does Brian write? He sets aside four months to work on each Redwall book. During these months, Brian writes intensively for about four to five hours a day. He usually writes by hand in a corner of the garden with his dog, Teddy, at his feet. "There's a connection between the brain, the arm, and the hand," Brian says of his preferred writing style. "I'm anti-technology, mate." He doesn't like using computers. He calls that just "pressing buttons and playing." He will sometimes use an old typewriter.

Writing in this style, Brian has given fans fourteen animal tales set in the medieval world of Redwall. He has no shortage of ideas. "If God spares me to live to be 250, I might get a quarter [of the books I want to write] out," he says.

Who's Your Favorite Author?

Steve Rowe
Age 13

*W*hen most think of a hero nowadays, they think big. I thought that too until I read *Redwall* by Brian Jacques. He reminded me that a hero could be nothing bigger than a mouse. He inspired me to think about things that you normally wouldn't, such as mice waving mystical silver swords and defeating the greatest evil to their kind.

Brian Jacques also taught me to think that anything is possible if you work hard enough at it. Matthias (the protagonist) was an orphan until one day when he knew he wanted to be a warrior mouse. Some other mice scoffed and said he would never be able to achieve it. But years of hard work, patience, and perseverance paid off, as he achieved his dream by defeating Cluny the Scourge and assuming the role. So the next time you think of heroes, you never know, the champion of the world might be in your own backyard.

Paula Danziger

Creating Write-On Characters

The cat ate my gymsuit.

Can you sue your parents for malpractice?

You can't eat your chicken pox, Amber Brown.

Everyone else's parents said yes.

*T*hese might sound like excuses, or overheard bits of conversation, but they're actually the wacky titles of some of Paula Danziger's books. With eye-catching titles like these, they're books you just have to read.

It's no surprise that Paula's books are as funny and clever as she is.

Since she was a girl, Paula has been writing. Writing was "always part of my life," she says. She spent most of her elementary school years on a Pennsylvania farm. Paula is allergic to animals, so her years spent on the farm were not her favorite time. But she did get her start as a writer during those years.

When Paula was eight years old, she created a newspaper with a neighborhood friend. She and her friend would write out each copy by hand (that was before the neighborhood copy stores). "Our hands usually got tired around ten copies."

They sold their newspapers for a nickel each. "That was the beginning of knowing that I loved writing," Paula says.

"I don't even remember what I wrote about. Isn't that awful?" she says with a laugh. But what she does remember is being a creative kid. Sometimes that got her in trouble at school.

"I used to get in a lot of trouble because I would have to do an assignment and I'd think the idea was really *boring*, so I would do it differently." For example, when Paula got an assignment for a research paper on life in the middle ages, she created a fake newspaper that covered stories set during that time. "Now kids do that all the time."

AMAZING...

The name of Paula's most popular character, Amber Brown, has nothing to do with the fact that Paula loves amber jewelry. She's a friend of Marc Brown, author of the Arthur books, and came up with the name as a funny suggestion for him when he and his wife were having a baby. (Get it? Amber is a shade of brown, so why not name the baby Amber Brown?) Marc didn't like the name. He was afraid the baby would be nicknamed "Crayola Face." Now her character Amber deals with that problem.

But True!

"I got a lot of A's over F's—A's for creativity, but F's for not doing the assignment correctly. The end result was lots of C's."

Paula not only liked to write, she also liked to read. When Paula's mom had to go to the grocery store, she would drop Paula off at the library to wait. Paula would check out a big stack of books and then have some of them read by the time her mom was through shopping. She read books from the Nancy Drew, Hardy Boys, and Bobbsey Twins series.

Try This

Paula says it's important to really know your characters when you write. Know everything about them, including what's in their closet, she says. Describe a character you might want to feature in a story. Start by describing what's in his or her closet. Remember, a closet is stocked with a lot more than just clothes.

In sixth grade, Paula and her family moved off the farm to Metuchen, New Jersey, a suburb not far from New York City. Her sixth-grade year was not a favorite chapter in her life. She was in a new home and a new school; and the teacher wasn't very nice, says Paula. In junior high, things got a little better.

Paula used a lot of her experiences growing up—both bad and good—in her first book, *The Cat Ate My Gymsuit*. Paula says Marcy Lewis, the thirteen-year-old star of the book, is her most autobiographical character. In the book, Marcy deals with being overweight, having a difficult dad, and standing up for what she believes.

Wise Words

We are all creative in our own way, no matter what we are going to be. My style is just a little more 'out there.'

That book is very important to Paula because she put so much of herself into the pages.

You'd never guess it today, but Paula says, in junior high, "I was shyer than most people would think."

By high school, she started expressing herself more and feeling more comfortable and confident.

"I was working on the school newspaper. I had lots of friends. I was happy."

Her friends discovered what readers know now: Paula has a great sense of humor. That sense of humor followed her to State Teachers College in New Jersey, where she worked on the campus humor magazine and eventually became the editor.

Paula's sense of style—spirited and fun—took off once she left home. Although she experimented with clothes in high school, her mom wanted her to stick to "clothes that matched." Once away from mom and dad, she was free to wear what she wanted. Today, if Paula comes to your school, she'll likely be wearing something fun or funky. Paula loves jewelry and usually wears ten rings on her fingers. "People really respond to my jewelry," she says.

Paula also loves fun footwear. She has a collection of Dr. Martens. One pair has landmarks from London painted on them. Another pair is covered with purple glitter. Paula is known for dressing with flair. "I love the fact that I put on little purple glitter shoes. They make me laugh. They make me smile in the morning."

Once she graduated from college, Paula had a variety of teaching jobs. She was a substitute teacher, a reading teacher, and taught in junior high for two years.

Then Paula was in a serious car accident and decided to stop teaching junior high students to pursue a master's degree in reading, with a focus on education. While she was working on her degree, she wrote her first book, *The Cat Ate My Gymsuit*.

Paula decided this was the right time in her life to get serious about being a writer. She based her book on her own experiences, writing about a kid with a family who didn't understand her and a teacher who was a little unusual and took political stands.

In *The Cat Ate My Gymsuit*, an English teacher, Ms. Finney, refuses to say the Pledge of Allegiance and is suspended. Paula wrote the book during the Vietnam War, when there were strong feelings about the United States being in the war. Ms. Finney is very popular with her students. She encourages

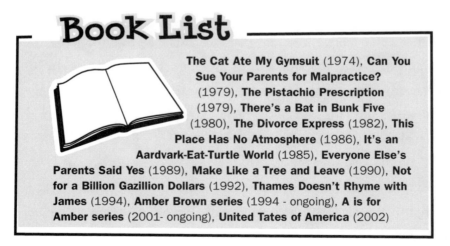

Book List

The Cat Ate My Gymsuit (1974), Can You Sue Your Parents for Malpractice? (1979), The Pistachio Prescription (1979), There's a Bat in Bunk Five (1980), The Divorce Express (1982), This Place Has No Atmosphere (1986), It's an Aardvark-Eat-Turtle World (1985), Everyone Else's Parents Said Yes (1989), Make Like a Tree and Leave (1990), Not for a Billion Gazillion Dollars (1992), Thames Doesn't Rhyme with James (1994), Amber Brown series (1994 - ongoing), A is for Amber series (2001- ongoing), United Tates of America (2002)

Where 2 Write

You can write to Paula at this address:

Paula Danziger
c/o Penguin Putnam
345 Hudson St.
New York, NY
10014-3657

Or you can read more about her at: **www.penguin putnam.com/amberbrown**

her students to be independent and creative thinkers. Paula was a teacher before writing the book, so you can imagine some of her experiences helped shape the character of Ms. Finney. Can you imagine how much fun it would be to have Paula as your teacher?

Paula shared that first book with her college professor, who also worked for a publishing company. He took the book to his publishing company and they bought it right away. The book was published in 1974.

She kept working and writing. "I'm a morning person, so I worked on writing mainly in the mornings and on weekends." She also wrote around her job at the college, because she wasn't sure she could support herself by writing alone.

After three books were published, she decided to make writing her full-time job. One of her most popular characters is Amber Brown, a smart, funny, and spunky girl who has to deal with her parents' divorce and the everyday ups-and-downs of elementary school life.

Some of Amber's personality is inspired by Paula's niece, Carrie. Paula came up with the idea for Amber after writing a short story for Carrie, who was sad about her best friend moving away. Paula decided to turn the story into a book, and

19

Amber Brown was born. Although the books are not about Carrie's life, Paula says, some of Carrie's flair and sense of style do show up in Amber's character. The book *You Can't Eat Your Chicken Pox, Amber Brown* was an idea that came from a trip Paula and Carrie took to England. Carrie really did get the chicken pox and a bird did poop in her hair, just like in the story.

Paula's family and New Jersey friends show up in her latest book, *The United Tates of America*, in photogaphs. This book follows the adventures of Skate Tate, a sixth-grader and scrap-booking fan.

Paula's been writing full-time for about twenty-five years now, with more than thirty books published. To keep on her writing schedule, she gets help from a

Personal Stuff

Born: August 18, 1944, in Washington, D.C.

Family: Paula is not married and has no children, but she is a cool aunt to her brother's four children.

Favorite books: As a girl, Paula loved series books like Nancy Drew, Bobbsey Twins, and the Hardy Boys.

Favorite color: Purple
Favorite foods: Sweets and sushi
Spends free time: Talking on the phone, reading, traveling, and shopping

Collections: Paula collects antique beaded bags, unusual jewelry, and books and artwork by her friends. She also has a giant sticker collection that she keeps on hand to decorate mail she sends to her fans. And she has a big collection of "ugly" salt and pepper shakers.

Awards: Paula's books have won many awards. Her favorite award is one she received in 1999 from the Educational Paperback Association. The award praised Paula for getting kids excited about reading.

writing friend by phone. That friend is Bruce Coville, author of many popular books, including the funny Alien series with titles like *Aliens Stole My Body* and *The Aliens Ate My Homework*. She and Bruce schedule a talk time on the phone almost every day when they're working on books. They read their work to each other over the phone and give each other suggestions and support. By setting daily talk time, they keep each other on schedule. "We've been doing this for a very long time," says Paula.

Paula isn't short on ideas for books. She recently launched a beginning reader series featuring Amber Brown in her early elementary years. Plus, Paula has more adventures planned for Amber, and for Skate Tate.

Does she have a favorite story? Nope. All of them are special to her.

"Anything I write is important to me or I wouldn't do it," says Paula.

Who's Your Favorite Author?

Kyrene Teipel

Age 10

*O*ne of my favorite authors is Paula Danziger. She writes the Amber Brown series. The whole series is great, but my favorite book in it is *Amber Brown is Not a Crayon*. I like Amber Brown because she's so true-to-life. The books don't have anything to do with magic or kings or queens or dragons or anything like that—it's just normal, real-life stuff about a normal girl. And yet, the books are so fascinating that you just can't put them down.

J. K. Rowling

Working Her Magic
with Books

J. K. Rowling is one amazing writer. But just as amazing as the stories she writes is her own life story.

Joanne Kathleen Rowling—known simply as J. K. Rowling by her fans—says she has never wanted to be anything but a writer. "From really early on, there was never anything else I wanted to do," says J. K.

The British writer was born in Chipping Sodbury, England, a place she credits for giving her an affection for unusual names. She wrote her first story when she was six. It was about a rabbit. "The rabbit got measles," recalled J. K.

J. K. not only liked to write, she loved to read. "My favorite book of all when I was a child was *The Little White Horse* by Elizabeth Goudge. It's probably the one book that's consciously influenced the Harry Potter books. Elizabeth Goudge always listed what the characters were eating; I really liked reading the lists of sandwiches. I don't know why, but I always found that really satisfying," says J. K. Another of her favorite authors was Louisa May Alcott, who wrote *Little Women*.

At school, she was good at most subjects, but her favorite was always English. "I was a lot like Hermione. She works very, very hard to compensate for feeling insecure and plain. I felt the same way. I was very unsporty—terrible at sports!"

"When I was twelve, I broke my arm playing net ball." J. K. describes net ball (a British and Australian game) as "basketball with all the excitement drained out of it."

J. K. calls Hermione "the brains of the outfit."

"I like her very, very much as a character," says J. K. "I felt there was a good, strong female lead." Hermione is very clever and smart.

Each of her main characters—Harry, his friends Ron

AMAZING...

Why J. K.? When she typed up her first manuscript, she put Joanne Rowling on it. Her British publisher phoned her and asked would she mind if they used her initials? It was a book that would appeal to boys but they "weren't sure boys would be that keen on picking up a book by a woman."

"That was a totally pointless exercise, disguising me. Two months after the book was published, I was on a very popular children's TV program, so pretty much every child knew. It doesn't seem to have made any difference at all."

But True!

Weasley and Hermione Granger—"all have their own particular qualities."

"Harry is bright, but he's not academic. He has to work hard in school. But Harry is able to fly well, and that's an important point to the story," says J. K.

"Without each other, they would never get as far as they do."

Harry was the character that J. K. always imagined. "Right from the start, his name was Harry," says J. K. Although Harry attends a boarding school, J. K. never went away to school.

When it came time to go to college, she went to Exeter University to study French, even though English was her best subject. "I still haven't figured that out," she says with a laugh.

After graduating with honors, J. K. took on several

Personal Stuff

Born: July 31, 1965, in Chipping Sodbury, England

Family: J. K. has a young daughter, Jessica, called Jessie. Jessie was born in 1993. J. K. lives with her husband, Neil Murray, near Edinburgh, Scotland.

Favorite reading: She started reading her daughter the first Harry Potter books when Jessie was six. "I was going to read them when she turned seven, but I caved in. She kept nagging and nagging. I thought it would make her feel more included because she's getting a lot of attention at school." They are also fans of Roald Dahl's *Charlie and the Chocolate Factory*.

Favorite sport to watch: Basketball
Pets: A guinea pig and a rabbit (both belong to Jessie)
Nickname: Friends call her Jo for short.

Favorite Harry Potter cover: J. K. likes the American versions by artist Mary GrandPre. The Dutch covers are her second favorite.

Honors and awards: *Harry Potter and the Philosopher's Stone* won the Smarties Book Prize Gold Award and the British Book Awards Children's Book of the Year in 1998.

jobs, including a job at Amnesty International, a human rights group, where she used her language skills.

So when did Harry enter her life? The idea for Harry came to J. K. in the summer of 1990. She had been apartment hunting in Manchester, England, and was on a train ride back to London. While riding on the train, the idea for a young wizard boy attending a special wizard school came to her suddenly. Throughout the ride, she thought about the boy. By the time her train pulled into the station, she had a rich and wonderful character fully formed in her mind. J. K. had invented Harry Potter, an orphan wizard-boy living with cruel and nasty human relatives who despise and mistreat him.

On the train ride, she also dreamed up many ideas for Hogwarts School of Witchcraft and Wizardry, and much of Harry's history. When she got home,

Try This

Whenever or wherever inspiration strikes, write your idea down! Remember, J. K. Rowling got the idea for her Harry Potter series when she was riding on a train. She didn't have a pen with her, so she spent her train ride thinking through the story. She raced home to make notes like crazy.

Be prepared for inspiration. Carry a notebook and pen with you, wherever you go. Jot down ideas, snatches of conversation, and favorite words or sayings you hear people using. That way you'll have a collection of ideas, words, and maybe even a brilliant idea for a story.

Wise Words

Resign yourself to the fact that you're going to write a lot of rubbish before you write something really good.

she scribbled notes like crazy. At the time, J. K. was working on her second novel for adults. She has never tried to get either of those novels published.

For the next few years, J. K. continued to make notes about "the most exciting idea" she'd ever dreamed up. She continued working at her job, doing research for Amnesty International.

About a year later, she moved to Portugal to teach English. There she met a Portuguese journalist and got married. She had a baby, Jessica, in 1993. But J. K.'s marriage wasn't working out. Soon after Jessica was born, J. K. and the baby left Portugal and moved to Scotland to be near her sister.

At that time, she wasn't living the best chapter of her life. She was a single mom, soon to be divorced. She even lived "on the dole" for a few months. (That's a British term for getting assistance from the government to help make ends meet.) But she doesn't like people to make a big deal of that part of

Where Write

You can write to J. K. at this address:

J. K. Rowling
c/o Scholastic Inc.
555 Broadway
New York, NY 10012-3999

You can read more about J. K. and her upcoming books at Scholastic's web site:
www.scholastic.com

Book List

Harry Potter and the Sorcerer's Stone (Scholastic, 1998), **Harry Potter and the Chamber of Secrets** (Scholastic, 1999), **Harry Potter and the Prisoner of Azkaban** (Scholastic, 1999), **Harry Potter and the Goblet of Fire** (Scholastic, 2000), **Quidditch Through the Ages by Kennilworthy Whisp** (actually by J. K.) (2001), **Fantastic Beasts & Where to Find Them by Newt Scamander** (actually by J. K.) (2001)

her life.

Finally, she was ready to write the book she'd been carrying around in her head for years.

She began to write her story in a neighborhood café. "I wasn't going to cafés to keep warm," she says. "You see, I was always writing in cafés, which most people didn't want to hear, because it takes some of the gloss off the rags-to-riches story. But I'd been writing in cafés for years and years and years—ten years before I finished Harry," she says.

Why? As a student and young woman, she always had flat-mates or roommates. If she was working in an office, she liked to spend her lunch hour writing. In a café, she could write uninterruptedly in a creative environment—plus someone else was making the coffee.

How did J. K. write her stories?

She wrote them by hand! "The first draft is still longhand. Then I type my first edit on the computer," says J. K. "I'm a fast typist!"

She loved the story so much, she couldn't bear to cut it—
even after three or four publishers turned down the first Harry
Potter book, saying, among other things, that it was far too
long for young readers.

"I didn't see how I could tell the story in fewer words," says
J. K. That's because she had mapped out the whole seven-book
series before the first book was published.

After hearing about that, a reporter once asked J. K. if she
knew in advance what the last word of the last book would be.
At the time, J. K. said the word would be "scar." "That could
change. I rewrite so much," says J. K.

Whatever the final word is, it's one Harry Potter fans will
be sorry to read. Saying good-bye to this favorite series will be
like saying good-bye to a great friend.

J. K. isn't sure she'll ever top Harry's stories, though she
will keep writing. "I'm utterly resigned that I will never write
anything as popular again," says J. K. "It's highly likely that I
will be forever known for Harry Potter. That's okay. I absolutely
put my heart and soul into Harry Potter."

Erin Neier
Age 9

My favorite author is J.K. Rowling. I have read all four Harry Potter books. J.K. has inspired me to use my imagination. I think that it would be cool to live in a wizarding world because of the invisible cloaks, Quidditch, and all the escapes to Hogsmeade Village, just outside of Hogwarts. She also inspired me to be Hermione, one of Harry's best friends, for Halloween. She has helped me to write better, my vocabulary has improved too.

I love being scared with books. That's exactly what Harry Potter books do to you. They scare you, teach you, and inspire you. Thank you J.K. Rowling for writing them!

Jack Gantos

A Journey Through His Journal

As a kid, Jack Gantos was always on the move. He was used to being the new kid in school.

He attended ten different schools in twelve years. He lived in Pennsylvania, Florida, North Carolina, and even Barbados!

Why did Jack move so often? That's what his family did. At first, his dad was in the Navy. Later, he was in the construction trade. Jack's dad was a "grass is always greener on the other side" kind of person, so he would go on to new projects that looked promising.

"Moving around never bothered my parents," says Jack. "Once my parents left Pennsylvania, they were really like tumbleweeds. There were times when the moving was perfectly fine, and it didn't bother me at all."

By the time Jack reached middle school, he was comfortable attending new schools, but it wasn't always easy. His mom was

Wise Words

> 66 Literature is meant to affect people's lives. Some people read the [Joey Pigza] book, and then write me a letter saying they knew a kid like Joey in their class who was driving everybody nuts. After reading the book, they say, 'We understand him better and are giving him a second chance.' To me, that's remarkable. I read these letters and think—what great kids! I wonder if I would have been that big-hearted. 99

very outgoing and made friends easily. His dad made friends at work. But for his older sister and him, the changes seemed hardest. For Jack, it got harder and harder to make new friends each time his family moved. To cope with all the changes, he stopped putting too much effort into being popular. He says he was never really in the popular crowd, but he got by.

"I always was quick at making a few friends—after all, there were plenty of people like me who were not so much looking to be popular, as they were looking to find other people with like-minded interests. I hung around kids who liked books, or with kids who were just interesting to me in some way," says Jack.

But Jack says he also learned how to be by himself. "Reading and writing were ways in which I could settle down, and reflect on who I was, what I liked, where I was going, what was driving me nuts, what made me laugh, what made me want to be good, what made me want to be bad—basically what made me define myself to myself."

With all the moves and changes, one constant in Jack's life was his journal. It was something he could pack up and take with him, even when the family moved to Barbados, an island

AMAZING...

Jack met Joey, the star of his popular and award-winning Joey Pigza books, in Lancaster, Pennsylvania. The boy sitting in the front row during one of Jack's school presentations wasn't really named Joey, but he gave Jack inspiration. Right in the middle of Jack's presentation, the boy screamed to his teacher, "I forgot to take my meds," and shot out the door to get his medicine for ADHD.

Jack says he has noticed a lot of kids with this disorder in schools over the years, but when he saw this boy, he knew he had a story. That student in Pennsylvania brought back memories of two of his childhood friends who were similar. It made him want to explore what life is like for a smart, funny kid who has to deal with the usual growing-up stuff, plus the challenges of ADHD. Inspiration struck and Joey Pigza was born. If you've read the Joey Pigza books, you know Joey too lives in Lancaster.

But True!

in the Caribbean Sea.

Jack got his first journal when he was in second grade. Why did he get a journal so young?

It wasn't because he was crazy about writing; after all, he was only in second grade. He got one because—like many little brothers—it was his job to copy his big sister in every way.

So when *she* got a journal, he says, he bugged, badgered, and begged his mom until he got one, too. He didn't do much with it during the first few years he had it, but by fifth or sixth grade, he was really hooked on writing in it.

"I started to see it as more of a lockbox. Something I could keep with me, something I could write in, confide in, draw in, and tape things in. It was sort of an all-purpose thing and I could keep it with me at all times."

He wrote about stuff that happened at home and at school.

Where 2 Write

You can write to Jack at this address:

Jack Gantos
c/o Children's Book Dept.
Farrar, Straus & Giroux
19 Union Square West
New York, NY 10003

Between the pages, he collected all kinds of stuff, like gum wrappers and ticket stubs. He even occasionally stuck something gross in there, like a bug. That served two purposes—for him it was something cool he wanted to keep, but it also kept his sister out of his journal.

"It was more like a scrapbook," Jack says.

He even drew pictures in it, like a map of the neighborhood. When he looks back at his journals, one item—or even a drawing—can bring memories flooding back.

Now he uses those journals as the starting place for creating his Jack Henry stories, tales based on Jack's own funny experiences and wacky adventures as a kid.

Jack still keeps a journal and even writes the first draft of his books in his notebooks before typing the stories into the

Try This

Keep a journal like Jack's. And we don't mean the kind your teacher assigns, in which you're forced to write on a particular topic. This is a journal for your eyes only. It's a place where you can write whatever you want—what you had to eat, to secrets, observations about your family, even your greatest hopes and dreams. Spelling doesn't matter—it's getting your thoughts down that's important. When Jack was growing up, his journal was in part a scrapbook where he stashed gum wrappers, ticket stubs, and newspaper articles about weird and curious stuff. If you want, why not do this too. You'll have a journal and scrapbook all in one.

computer to edit and polish.

Are the stories from his journals true? Yup. At least mostly true.

The great thing about writing stories is that you can take things a little further than real life and have fun with the dialogue, Jack says. "I've given Betsy some blistering dialogue in the books," he says. But in real life, "Betsy" is his sister Karen, and she's not at all mean. At least not anymore. "Oh, she's a cupcake. She's sweet," Jack says with a chuckle. Why didn't he use his sister's name in the book? At first, Karen didn't think she'd like that.

His little brother, Alex, became Pete in Jack's stories. But his other brother, Eric, let Jack use his name. After his first book about his family was published, everyone decided they wanted their real names in the book.

But, of course, it was too late. Jack did use his own real name, at least his first name, in the Jack Henry stories. Just like Jack Henry, Jack always managed to get along, no matter what adventure came his way. Jack got along fine in school, but he was still relieved when he graduated. He was all set to go to college in Florida but felt it would be just too much like high school. He needed a break, so he took about three years to work for his dad's construction company. Jack didn't mind hard work, but he knew he wouldn't stay in construction—he wanted to have a job that he *really* loved.

Jack had seen enough people doing jobs they didn't even like. "People were doing jobs to make money, but they weren't necessarily happy about it," says Jack. That observation made a lasting impression on Jack. He knew that whatever he chose to do with his life, the job had to be something he would love to do.

Book List

Rotten Ralph series (1976 - 2001), **Heads or Tails: Stories from the Sixth Grade** (1994), **Jack's New Power: Stories From a Caribbean Year** (1995), **Desire Lines** (1997), **Jack's Black Book** (1997), **Joey Pigza Swallowed the Key** (1998), **Jack on the Tracks** (1999), **Joey Pigza Loses Control** (2000), **Hole in My Life** (2002), **What Would Joey Do?** (2002)

That goal led him to writing. After years of writing journals, it was one thing he knew he loved. He ended up at Emerson College in Boston, where he earned a degree in creative writing.

Even before he got his degree, Jack started writing picture books, including his first Rotten Ralph book, which was published when he was a junior in college.

By the time he graduated, he had two picture books published and two more finished and ready to be published. The first year after college, he stayed in Boston, living at a rooming house as a boarder for $25 a week. He was earning enough money from the royalties (author's payments) from his picture books to take a year off and

Personal Stuff

Born: July 2, 1951, in Mt. Pleasant, Pennsylvania

Family: Jack lives in Boston with his wife, Ann, and daughter, Mabel.

On the road: Jack loves to visit schools and talk to kids. He's visited more than 500 schools in the past ten years.

Free time: He loves spending time with his family, working out, and eating good food. Jack says, "I only exercise to eat good food."

Favorite reading: As a kid, Jack loved history, biographies, science fiction, and books about baseball and racecars. He was a big fan of the Hardy Boys series. Jack now spends a lot of time reading to Mabel. She's a Rotten Ralph fan, but she finds Ralph a bit scary at times. Her favorite stories are the ones Jack tells her about his growing-up years; especially the time his big sister, Karen, locked him outside when he was naked!

Honors and awards: *Joey Pigza Swallowed the Key* was a National Book Award finalist, an ALA Notable Book of the Year, and a School Library Journal Best Book of the Year. *Joey Pigza Loses Control* was named a Newbery Honor book.

really work on his writing. He went to the Boston Public Library every day to read and write.

Eventually, Jack became a college teacher and taught other writers. Though Jack enjoyed his job, he wanted to write full-time, so he quit in 1995, after the first of the Jack Henry stories, *Heads or Tails,* was published.

"It was a big decision," Jack says of leaving the teaching job that he loved, but it didn't give him enough time to write. He moved to New Mexico for a few years and, more recently, back to Boston.

What's his writing life like now? Jack is an early riser. On good days, he gets up at 5 A.M. and writes for two hours. He still writes in his personal journal every day, and he also writes the first draft of his stories in a journal, using notebooks and writing longhand. Later, he types his stories into his computer. He makes time for breakfast with his wife, Ann, and daughter, Mabel, and then helps get Mabel off to school. By 9 A.M., it's back to writing until lunchtime.

He takes an afternoon break to do chores or to work out; he's at his computer again from 3 - 5 P.M. Those afternoon hours are usually filled with rewriting or editing his work.

Jack says he rewrites a lot. Some chapters may be revised twenty times!

Not all of Jack's stories are based on his journals or his boyhood adventures. In 1998, Jack introduced us to a wonderful character, Joey Pigza, in the book *Joey Pigza Swallowed the Key.* That and his other books about a boy with Attention Deficit Hyperactivity Disorder (ADHD) have won several awards.

Jack isn't finished with his Jack Henry stories, either. He's working on a story about his family's move to Cape Hatteras, North Carolina, when he was in fourth grade. Jack laughs and says with a smile that despite the stress of the many moves, he's grateful his parents picked fun and exotic places to live.

But for now, Jack is right at home in Boston, writing away!

Who's Your Favorite Author?

Dexter Blumenthal
Age 9

Why would Joey Pigza think of swallowing the key and jumping from the highest rafter of an Amish farmer's barn? Who could take such crazy ideas and turn them into books you can't put down? The answer, of course, is Mr. Jack Gantos, the author of the stories of Jack Henry and Joey Pigza.

Reading Jack Gantos switches on all of your senses. His vivid descriptions set you on edge and bring the action off the page like a pop-up book. In *Joey Pigza Swallowed the Key,* when he describes Joey eating the shoofly pie and running through the corn-field to the barn, I could taste the sugary aftertaste of the molasses in my mouth, smell the fresh cornstalks, feel the wind and long curved leaves slicing up my arms. I could see the barn in the distance against the backdrop of the blue sky and feel just how totally out of control Joey was as he ran. I felt just like Joey, an incredible energy building inside me, and I couldn't help but want to yell, "Joey, stop!" because I knew that something bad was going to happen.

Christopher Paul Curtis

Driven to Write

*T*he road to writing for Christopher Paul Curtis had lots of twists and turns. For someone who loves cars, maybe that wasn't a bad thing.

Making a career out of writing wasn't something his family or friends in Flint, Michigan, ever talked about when he was a kid. Building cars was what Christopher and his classmates figured they'd do when they grew up—just like many of their fathers did.

Christopher's home—a small, cozy house in an auto-factory town—was filled with kids, car talk, and lots of books. Christopher's dad was trained to be a chiropodist, or doctor who specializes in treating feet.

Mr. Curtis was planning to open a practice in Flint, but Christopher played a part in changing those plans. "You could say he switched to the auto work because of me," says Christopher. It was just about the time "I was coming along," says Christopher, that his dad decided to make a career change.

The auto business was booming and jobs in the Flint auto plants were "good jobs with dignity." For his dad, Herman, who became an autoworker and United Auto Workers union leader, it was a good job for raising a family. Christopher's mom, Leslie, was also college-educated like his dad, but stayed home to raise the kids. Both his parents were huge readers. Every room in the house had books. Encyclopedias, storybooks, biographies, and novels were on the shelves. "I was a very good reader," says Christopher. "My parents were avid readers—we were always around books. I loved to read."

When he wasn't at home or at school, Christopher was usually at the library, even if he had no homework to research. "I'd go to the library and look at books—especially on the Civil War," he remembers. He loved to pore over the stories of soldiers and long-ago battles.

He also logged many hours reading comic books and magazines. But what Christopher couldn't find at the library—and this has shaped his writing today—were books for boys. Especially African-American boys like him.

What was life like at the Curtis house?

Where Write

You can write to Christopher at this address:

**Christopher Paul Curtis
c/o Random House
Children's Books
1540 Broadway
New York, NY 10036**

and **kids@randomhouse.com**

You can also read about Christopher Paul Curtis at:
www.randomhouse.com

Book List

The Watsons Go To Birmingham (1995), **Bud, Not Buddy** (1999), **Bucking the Sarge** (2002)

There was fun, but there were also rules to follow. For example, Christopher had to be in bed early, but he was allowed to stay awake longer if he was reading in bed.

In school, Christopher was smart and liked to learn. He has a vivid memory of playing a word game in second grade. Every week, his teacher would take a long word like "democracy" and see how many other words students could make from the letters in it. Whoever came up with the most words was the winner. Winning that game netted Christopher his first prize ever—a candy bar.

Christopher was a whiz at the game, and the reward was sweet. But it was just a tiny taste of what was to come. Christopher enjoyed writing throughout school, but being a writer for a job? That wasn't Christopher's plan. When high school graduation rolled around, he told his parents, "I want to work in the car factory."

Christopher says, "I just didn't think you could make a living being a writer." Everyone says you can't make any money at it, so it didn't seem practical, he says. "The idea of work then was that you have to sweat, get dirty, and work real hard."

His decision caused a bit of a fight between his parents. His dad figured factory work paid well and "would make a man" out of Christopher.

"My dad thought if I worked in the factory, I'd see how rough it was and then I'd want to go to school."

"My mom," says Christopher, "was afraid if I started work-

AMAZING...

One of the benefits of being a famous writer is that Christopher gets to travel around the country, occasionally meeting interesting people. A few years ago, he went to New York City and was introduced to the actress Whoopi Goldberg. Whoopi purchased the rights to make a movie out of his book *The Watsons Go to Birmingham*. (Those rights have since been sold to another company for possible TV series development.) Whoopi knew Christopher's daughter, Cydney, was coming and brought her a gift—a Whoopi doll that the actress got when she was promoting a Japanese candy.

Christopher loved meeting Whoopi, but laughs at the memory of his daughter's reaction to the doll. Christopher describe the doll like this: "It had somewhat of a broken neck with the head hanging to the side. When you clapped your hands, the doll started to walk. It walked like Frankenstein's monster with a broken neck. And it said something like, 'Chew, chew, swallow.'" Cydney was terrified of the doll. Once the doll was home, the batteries were taken out and it was put away under Christopher's bed. "I never dreamed I'd be traveling around the country talking about a book I wrote. I never dreamed I'd have a Whoopi Goldberg doll hiding under my bed at home. But I do."

But True!

ing in the factory and started making money, I wouldn't want to go to school."

So which parent turned out to be right? When Christopher shares this story at presentations, he asks everyone in his audience to guess the answer to that question.

His mom was right. Christopher remembers that with his first paycheck he bought a cool 8-track cassette player with huge speakers. "The next thing I brought was a brand new 1972 Camaro," Christopher says. "I don't like to brag, but I looked REEALLY good driving it."

Soon after that, Christopher got his own apartment.

"For the first time in my life, girls started going out with me," he says with a laugh. Christopher liked his

Personal Stuff

Born: May 10, 1954, in Flint, Michigan

Family: Christopher lives with his wife Kaysandra and their daughter Cydney, near Windsor, Ontario. Their son Steven is grown up.

Free time: Christopher loves to play basketball and listen to music. He keeps a collection of records and CDs, especially jazz. He also loves to spend time with his family.

Favorite foods: Mexican, West Indian, and Indian

Favorite reading: As a boy, Christopher liked to read *Mad* magazine and other comic books, newspapers, and sports magazines. He also loved history books, especially about the Civil War. Today, he loves anything by Toni Morrison, Zora Neale Hurston, or Kurt Vonnegut.

Awards and honors: *Bud, Not Buddy* won the Newbery award and the Coretta Scott King Award in 2000, and received the American Library Association Best Book for Young Adults honor.

Wise Words

What's the hardest part of writing? Editing. That's the least interesting part, but it is the most important part.

new life. He had his own place, a cool car, and a big sound system. Who could want more? "I kept getting in deeper and deeper. I was supposed to go [to the factory] for three months and save my money for college. I ended up being there thirteen years!"

The three-month timeline was mainly his mom's idea. "She thought I'd get a taste of the work and that would be that." By then, Christopher had started buying stuff—like his car. And he was hooked on earning that paycheck.

Although he liked the money, he hated every minute of the job. But he believes it was working at the factory that finally turned him into a writer.

So just what was his job? Christopher was a door hanger at Flint Fisher Body Plant #1. The work was sweaty and tough. He hung 300 doors a day, each weighing 50 to 80 pounds, onto Buicks as they rolled down the assembly line. He was definitely using his muscles, but he was using his brain as well.

Christopher came up with a great way to fit writing into his job on the assembly line. Instead of alternating hanging doors with a co-worker in fifteen-minute shifts, he worked out a deal: he'd do the doors for thirty minutes, and then take a thirty-minute break.

"It was during that half-hour break that I started to write," he says. "I was lucky. I found out if I wrote during that time, my work day would go by very quickly." He built writing time into his day.

While Christopher was hanging doors, he imagined what he'd write on his next break. "I wasn't writing fiction at that time. I was mostly writing my experiences," he says.

He didn't know it then, but that was the beginning of his life as a famous writer. He also began taking classes at the Flint campus of the University of Michigan.

Working in the factory and writing during his breaks was good discipline. Christopher wanted to write something every day to make the time go by faster. But getting published didn't happen overnight. He spent thirteen years working in the factory, writing and going to classes. During that time, Christopher also got married and started a family.

Just as the factory work helped Christopher become a writer, Kaysandra, his future wife, helped him improve his

Try This

Christopher Paul Curtis says, "Learn your history." He was inspired by family stories. Some of the stories that he heard at family reunions later became inspiration for his books. Set aside an hour to interview someone in your family about events in your family's history. Ask them ahead of time to bring photos or family souvenirs. After your interview, write a story based on what you learned. Even if you never become a published author, this will be a wonderful keepsake.

writing skills. While they were dating, Kaysandra lived in Canada and Christopher lived in Flint, Michigan. At first, Christopher made lots of weekend road trips. But after many miles, his sporty Camaro conked out, and he couldn't make the weekend road trips anymore. He was forced to win her heart by mail.

So Christopher began writing letters—lots and lots of letters. He worked, wrote, and wooed his girlfriend. After piles of romantic letters, the two got married. Christopher kept writing. And soon, he got his big break.

Was it from a book publisher? Nope, once again, it was from Kaysandra. Christopher loves to tell the story when he speaks to groups. "Kay told me the three magic words—those three magic words that made me feel warm and bubbly and meant everything."

"'I love you?'" suggests Christopher.

No, it was even better. "The words were: 'Take off work.'"

Christopher decided to do just that. Kaysandra, a nurse, said she would support the family—they had two children by then—while Christopher focused on writing. Christopher went right back to his favorite place—the library—to get started on his first book. A quiet corner surrounded by books was just the place for Christopher to sit down and write.

Remember, though, Christopher was used to factory hours. He was his own boss now, but he stayed on schedule, just like he was going to his old job. He got up at 5 A.M., ate breakfast, and did an hour or two of rewriting on his work before heading to the library. Then, with a pencil and a pad of paper, he wrote.

And wrote. And wrote.

What did he write about? He'd had a story kicking around in his head for some time. He had used parts of it in shorter stories for his college classes. The story was a mix of his family history, his imagination, and historic facts about the 1960s.

This mix eventually became *The Watsons Go to Birmingham*. Christopher entered the story in a book-publishing contest. He finally got the phone call he'd been waiting for: "The editor called to tell me I had . . . LOST! That hurt my feelings."

But the good news was that the editor liked the story so much that the publishing company wanted to publish it anyway. He was offered a contract and—zoom!—Christopher was on his way to becoming a famous writer. He celebrated with his whole family.

Confident now that he could write for a living, Christopher began his second book, *Bud, Not Buddy*. This book was set in the 1930s, during the Great Depression, and like his first book, wove history into fiction. In *Bud, Not Buddy*, he used his real-life family as inspiration. One grandfather, Herman F. Curtis, was a bandleader for the Dusky Devastators of the Depression. And another grandfather, Earl "Lefty" Lewis, was a pitcher for a Grand Rapids baseball team. Their stories inspired two of the characters in the book. "I think it's really important to listen to the stories they [your family] share. You can check out a book about the Depression [or any historical topic], but when you have someone who's been there, ask questions." Christopher heard many stories when the family gathered for reunions.

Where else does Chris get ideas for his stories? He says he

has no magic formula. On those days when he goes to the library, "Sometimes I just sit and wait for the story to come to me." Even though he's now a famous author, he continues to go to the library to write. Then he types the story into the computer and does all his editing on the computer at home. A few years ago, when he was just getting started, his son Steven helped with the computer. Today Steven is away in the Navy, but Christopher sends him early drafts of his books in progress to get his opinion.

Christopher's daughter, Cydney, has helped, too. Christopher loves to tell the story of Cydney's made-up song, "Mommy Says No." When he was writing *Bud, Not Buddy*, Cydney sang a very short song she had just composed in her head. He thought the song was so funny that he used it in his book, giving Cydney a credit as the song's author.

His third novel, *Bucking the Sarge*, is about a fifteen-year-old boy who works in a group home that his mother runs. His mom wants him to take over her property business—she's also a landlord with rental properties—but he's more of a philosopher. He's been helping her as a health-care aide since sixth grade, so he doesn't have many friends.

This book is for slightly older readers. But fans of *Bud, Not Buddy* can look forward to a companion novel—not quite a sequel, but a parallel story, says Christopher, also taking place during the Depression. This story is seen through the eyes of Deza Malone, the girl whom Bud first locked lips with at Hooverville, the camp outside of Flint.

Meanwhile, a film company has bought the rights to make *Bud, Not Buddy* into a movie. While the idea of seeing his story on the big screen is exciting, Christopher's first love is writing.

His second is reading. If you want to know where Christopher is most days, he's at the library—always one of his favorite places.

It's a place he recommends for all would-be writers. A place to read, write, and think. It's not a place where you have to be in a hurry.

If you want to be a writer, slow down. You've got plenty of time. "Be patient," says Christopher. After all, he spent thirteen years writing while he worked at another job, before he wrote his first book.

Unlike cars, books can't be produced on an assembly line. Each book is custom-made, with its own special style and features. That's true of Christopher's award-winning stories, too. Each one is made to last and destined to be a classic.

Kayla Jamieson
Age 12

Christopher Paul Curtis wrote my favorite book, *Bud, Not Buddy.* Bud is my most favorite character because he is very brave for trying to find what he really wanted in life. I like this character because he went through many obstacles and troubles, but he did not stop believing he could make it. I always had my nose in this book. Every time I read something interesting, I would tell someone and encourage him or her to read it. My sister is the one who encouraged me to read *Bud, Not Buddy.* She read parts of it to me before she went to bed. I liked it so much I read it myself. I wish there were a series of books about Bud. This is a great book and I really encourage you to read it.

Louis Sachar

Digging Up Good Stories

*W*hat do Louis Sachar and Michael Jordan have in common? Both faced rejection in high school at the things that have made them famous today. Everybody knows the story of Michael Jordan being cut the first time he tried out for his high school basketball team. But did you know that Louis Sachar, the writer of the award-winning book *Holes*, was turned away from the high school newspaper after his writing sample didn't measure up?

Just like Michael, Louis didn't let rejection stop him.

Louis began elementary school in East Meadow, New York, but his family made a big move—heading all the way to Tustin, California—when he was nine years old.

Louis remembers being excited about the move. Like a lot of kids his age, his first thought was "Disneyland! We could go to Disneyland!" And yes, Louis did go to Disneyland—his family lived only ten miles away from the theme park. But once he was in the fourth grade and settled, growing up in California was like growing up anywhere. Like most kids, he was caught up in the daily routine of school and family life. "Once I was there in California, I didn't think about what might make it different," says Louis.

At school, Louis was good at math—in fact, he was good at most school subjects.

He was smart—and knew how to be funny.

"I was a bit of a class clown," says Louis. Anyone who has read the hilarious Wayside School stories isn't surprised. But, says Louis, "I could never be as funny in person as in writing. In writing, you can make it perfect. When you're talking, you may say something that sounds stupid."

Louis, like the rest of his family, was a big reader. But, says Louis, his older brother was the one who people thought was the talented writer in the family. After high school, Louis went

Book List

There's a Boy in the Girls' Bathroom (1987), **Marvin Redpost: Kidnapped at Birth?** (1992), Dogs Don't Tell Jokes (1992), **Marvin Redpost: Why Pick on Me?** (1993), **Marvin Redpost: Is He a Girl?** (1993), **Marvin Redpost: Alone in His Teacher's House** (1994), **The Boy Who Lost His Face** (1997), **Marvin Redpost: Class President** (1999), **Marvin Redpost: A Flying Birthday Cake?** (1999), **Holes** (1998), **Super Fast: Out of Control** (2000), **A Magic Crystal** (2000)

to college. He headed to the University of California at Berkeley. Louis had a dream of being a writer, but figured that wasn't a way he could make a living. His plan was simple: "I figured I would get a job and maybe con- tinue to write on the side."

One of the courses he took in college involved being a teacher's aide. "I signed up because I thought it looked like a good way to earn three credits senior year," says Louis. He was sent to nearby Hillside Elementary School. Louis was surprised by how much he liked the job. He even took an added job at the school as a paid supervisor during lunch recess.

Personal Stuff

Born: March 20, 1954, in East Meadow, New York

Family: Louis lives with his wife, Carla, and teenage daughter, Sherre, in Austin, Texas

Hobbies: Louis is a huge fan of the game of bridge and a com- petitive player. When he's not writing, he likes to travel to bridge tournaments around the country. He also likes to jog, ski, and play tennis.

Favorite books: His favorites were books about animals and sports. He regularly ordered books through the school book club. In high school, two favorites were J. D. Salinger and Kurt Vonnegut.

Honors and awards: Louis's book *Holes* has received the Newbery Medal, National Book Award, and the School Library Journal Best Book of the Year.

That job, supervising kids, turned out to be the most valuable job of Louis's life. But he didn't know that at the time.

After college, Lewis got a job in a sweater warehouse. He was a manager in charge of filling out shipping orders, among other things. He wrote when he wasn't filling sweater orders. But the warehouse didn't have enough work and soon Louis was out of a job. "I had to figure out what I could do," says Louis. "So I figured I would try law school."

In the meantime, he kept writing. He had been working on a story that first to came to him when he was a lunch supervisor. It was on the playground that he got his ideas for the *Sideways Stories from Wayside School* series. The kids of Wayside School are all named after kids from the school where he worked.

He even used the nickname students had for him—Louis the Yard Teacher. He also used some of the characteristics of real teachers from his school to make up the wonderful and wacky staff at Wayside School.

While he was sending out applications to law school, Louis was also sending publishers the manuscript for his first school story.

He heard first from law school and was accepted. Then, the first week of law school, he heard from the last publisher he had sent the story to. After several rejections, a publishing company was offering him a contract.

He was thrilled—but he didn't think he should quit law

AMAZING...

When writing *Holes*, Louis couldn't think of a last name for Stanley. So he made it Yelnats (Stanley spelled backwards) in an early draft. Louis says he was going to change it in one of his rewrites, but decided not to. Did you notice that?

But True!

Try This

Look at rewriting as just another form of writing, not hard work. Louis puts it this way: "It's like doing a sculpture of a person, you put the legs and arms and head on, then you go back and give features to the face and make the arms more natural-looking, and . . . every time you go back shaping your sculpture, it looks more like a person, less like a lump of clay." Take one of your recent writing assignments and go after it like Michelangelo—and see if rewriting and polishing can turn your work into a masterpiece.

school. He still wasn't sure he could make a full-time living writing stories for kids.

Luckily, those school stories became a huge hit. He still remembers all the fan mail—which helped him decide that he could finally take a chance on writing for a living. He did finish law school, but he never became a lawyer.

Instead, for nearly twenty years, he's been writing full-time.

What's his secret? Hard work. "The first few days are the hardest," says Louis. "Sometimes I just sit at the computer until an idea comes."

His wife, Carla, and daughter, Sherre, know better than to interrupt him—or to ask how the book is going. But they do inspire him. Both Carla and Sherre have influenced Louis's characters. The sister in the Marvin Redpost series has a slight resemblance to Sherre, and his wife, Carla, was the inspiration for the counselor in *There's a Boy in the Girls' Bathroom*. She was a school counselor when they met.

Louis is a very disciplined writer and tries to stick to a regular schedule. Most days he starts the morning with a jog, or fast walk with his two Australian shepherd dogs, Lucky and Tippy. After breakfast, he heads to his home office where he spends two to three hours at the computer for solid writing time. Lucky and Tippy are asleep at his feet while he's writing.

"The first draft is the hardest to me." But he says, you have to get something—anything—down.

If Louis needs a break, he plays with an old pinball machine in the office. Louis says that after about three hours of writing, he's "lost the freshness." He takes a quick break.

Then it's back to the computer. "Once you've written it, now you've got something—something to build on."

Louis spends lots of time rewriting and reworking those first ideas. He usually does five to six rough drafts before the story is shipped to his editor.

When Louis talks about rewriting, he gets excited. He will turn chapters upside down, change characters, and rethink whole ideas in the rewrite process. That's the fun part of writing for him.

How does he come up with his ideas?

"That's a mystery to me," says Louis. "But when an idea comes,"

Where Write

You can write to Louis at this address:

**Louis Sachar
c/o Random House
Children's Books
1540 Broadway
New York, NY 10036**

Louis says, "it just comes very suddenly."

The award-winning *Holes* started with a story setting and a name.

Louis wanted to try something different than the regular school settings of his earlier books. "Camp Green Lake" came to him suddenly. The setting was influenced, says Louis, by the hot and dry Texas summers. (Usually Louis and his family try to leave Texas during the hottest part of the summer.) Choosing the setting first was an exception for Louis. Most of the time, he says, his stories start with the characters.

Camp Green Lake is a hot, dusty place with no lake in sight. The camp is a camp for bad boys and their main punishment is digging holes—lots of holes—in the hot Texas sun. The main character, Stanley Yelnats, is sent there for a crime he didn't commit. What happens at the camp to Stanley and some of the other unforgettable characters makes for a strange and wonderful story. It's much different than any of the earlier books. There is some funny stuff—but the tale is serious and mysterious. *Holes* is an amazing story.

Soon, *Holes* will be a movie. Louis turned his book into a screenplay (a movie script)—a whole different kind of writing.

Wise Words

> " When I rewrite, I'm rethinking. I make great changes. I couldn't even begin to list them. It's dramatic. I know I'll change great portions of a story when I rewrite. "

What's next? Louis is busy writing another book. But he never talks about his next project, explaining that he has a rule on never spilling the beans about a book before it's published. Another reason Louis doesn't share much about his future books is that he can turn a tale topsy-turvy before it's in final form.

But whatever form it takes, it's sure to be great!

Domanique Nichols
Age 10

My very favorite book character is Stanley Yelnats, from *Holes* by Louis Sachar. I read the book in school and really liked it. I love the character Stanley because he is smart, confident, and honest. I think it was awesome how he broke his family's curse and also taught Zero to read. This book was awesome.

Patricia Polacco

Her Life Is An Open Book

*W*hen Patricia Polacco was a little girl, she wanted to be a ballet dancer. In fact, she took lessons for many years.

She never dreamed she'd grow up to be a famous author and illustrator. But she did!

Patricia has overcome many obstacles in order to become a writer, including learning disabilities called dyslexia (dis-LEX-ee-ah) and dysnumeria (dis-nu-MER-ee-ah), which very few people understood when Patricia was in school. Patricia explains dyslexia like this: "It's when the brain will change what the eyes see." Dysnumeria, says Patricia, is a disability that made it nearly impossible for her to do math problems, although she could understand the concept. Her brain processes the information differently, making math a struggle.

If you've read Patricia's book, *Thank You, Mr. Falker,* you know about her struggle with words. The book is a tribute to her real-life teacher, Mr. Felker, who helped her understand why reading and writing were so difficult. In real life, Patricia was fourteen when Mr. Felker helped her understand her learning disability, but because she wanted to tell the story in a picture book for younger readers, the main character discovers her learning disability in fifth grade. In this story, she shares her memories of being ruthlessly teased for years in elementary school. Once Patricia got the help she needed, she did well in school. She finished high school and went to college, eventually earning a graduate degree in art history.

Where Write

You can write to Patricia at this address:

**Patricia Polacco
118 Berry St.
Union City, MI 49094**

You can visit Patricia online at:

www.patriciapolacco.com

Patricia was born in Lansing, Michigan, the state's capital city. She lived in Williamston, and then Union City, both small farming communities near Lansing. Her parents divorced when she was three, and she divided her time between her dad and grandparents in Williamston, and her mom and grandparents in Union City.

Though her parents didn't stay married, Patricia feels she was lucky to have a good relationship with both parents and with her loving grandparents, who helped take care of her and enrich her life. Patricia's books are filled with stories about her family heritage and the rich traditions that shaped her life. Her mother's family came to the United States from the Ukraine and Russia. They were Jewish. Her dad's family was from Ireland. They were Christian. If you visited Patricia's house in December, you'd see that she celebrates traditions from both families. She has many Hanukkah menorahs and a Christmas tree in just about every room. Those cultures both value the sharing of tales, especially passing down stories between generations.

Stories have always come easy to Patricia. Many of her tales come from her childhood, but she's also got a great imagination, which she says comes from growing up in two houses filled with storytellers and creative people. Her dad was a co-host on a TV talk show. Her mom was a teacher and jazz pianist. Her parents and her grandparents were all excellent storytellers.

One story that comes from Patricia's family is *The Keeping Quilt*. The story is about a special quilt that has been passed

Book List

Meteor! (1987), **The Keeping Quilt** (1988), **Boat Ride with Lillian Two Blossom** (1988), **Rechenka's Eggs** (1989), **Thunder Cake** (1990), **Chicken Sunday** (1992), **The Bee Tree** (1993), **Babushka Baba Yaga** (1993), **My Rotten Redheaded Older Brother** (1994), **Pink and Say** (1994), **Babushka's Mother Goose** (1995), **I Can Hear The Sun** (1996), **In Enzo's Splendid Garden** (1997), **Thank You, Mr. Falker** (1998), **Mrs. Mack** (1998), **Luba and the Wren** (1999), **Welcome Comfort** (1999), **The Butterfly** (2000), **Betty Doll** (2001), **Mr. Lincoln's Way** (2001), **When Lightning Comes in a Jar** (2002) down from generation to generation. The quilt is created to help homesick Anna, Patricia's great-grandma, remember the old country when she first comes to America. Anna's mother uses material from the dress Anna wore when she emigrated to this country—but has outgrown—and her *babushka* (a Russian scarf) to create a keepsake that will help her remember family back home.

The keeping quilt is also made of scraps of fabric from other family members' clothing. "My grandmother told my mother about all the pieces and who they belonged to," says Patricia. She remembers that the quilt was part of every family celebration. She even used the quilt as a cape to play Superman. Today, through the book, many readers know about how the quilt came to be and how it's been used in Patricia's own family. Her parents wrapped her in the quilt when she was born, and she wrapped her children, Traci and Steven (now grownups) in the

AMAZING...

Patricia Polacco did not fully learn to read until she was fourteen. That's after she found out she had dyslexia. In her picture book, *Thank you, Mr. Falker*, she writes about a fifth-grade girl who learns to read thanks to a sensitive and smart teacher. It's Patricia's own story. She changed the age of the girl because she wanted to reach younger readers who might be dealing with the same problem. On her book jacket, she says, "Maybe the children who read this book will remember to say thank you to all those teachers they have loved."

But True!

quilt when they were babies.

When Patricia's mom moved, Patricia and her brother joined her. They went to Florida for a few years and then to a home in Oakland, California. That's where Patricia attended school and where she spent most of her growing-up years. But she came home every summer to visit her dad in Michigan.

Patricia says she loved Oakland because "it was a place where people of many backgrounds, many faiths and ideas lived." Patricia feels this experience was an important one. As a girl growing up in Oakland, she made lifelong friends, including her best friend, Stewart Washington. They were friends and neighbors for thirty years.

Now that Patricia is living in Michigan, they are long-distance best friends, but Stewart does come to visit. One of Patricia's books, *Chicken Sunday*, is dedicated to Stewart and tells a tale of how they raised money to buy Stewart's grandma, Eula Mae, a special Easter bonnet. Because Stewart is often on Patricia's mind, she has used him as a model for characters in her books, including the cool principal in *Mr. Lincoln's Way*. In real life, Stewart is an actor and an electrician.

Although Patricia has many happy memories of growing up in Oakland, she had some unhappy times in school. Though she was extremely creative from an early age, she struggled with math, reading, and writing. Luckily, her parents encouraged her other gifts—including her wonderful drawing style.

When she was just three, she could draw "pictures that would make your jaw drop." By the time she was five, she was making little picture books for her family. "My early books

Try This

Patricia was lucky to have two sets of grandparents, both actively involved in her life and both with a legacy of story-telling.

Take time to find out about your family's stories. Talk to your mom, dad, grandparents, or an aunt or uncle about their growing-up years. Maybe pick up a favorite item, like a teacup, and ask them to tell you about it. Chances are you'll learn something you didn't know. Write down what you learn.

were like hieroglyphics," Patricia says. "But you could follow along. You knew exactly what was going on in the story."

Patricia hid her school struggles for years. When she was in seventh grade, with the help of Mr. Felker, she discovered that she had learning disabilities. Those learning disabilities made her a frequent target of taunts and harassment from the school bully.

What's it like to be bullied and picked on? Patricia has never forgotten. Not only does she write about bullying, she often travels to schools across the country to speak about the problem. She still can remember the name of her tormentor.

Says Patricia, "I let kids know what it's like to be inside my skin—and feel dumb and stupid. The other side of it is that I tell any learning-disabled student in the room that they are probably geniuses."

She knows how hard kids are on themselves. As a child,

Patricia felt like everybody was perfect, except for her. She thought something was wrong with her.

That wouldn't have happened if all kids respected each other's skills and talents. Teaching kids to be kind and respectful of each other has become her mission. "We need to be aware of being gentler and kinder to each other," says Patricia. Not only does Patricia remember the person who made her life so miserable in school, she also remembers a friend who was picked on and went on to become a successful artist and performer—eventually working in the television and movie industry.

He was a friend in high school and used puppets to combat bullying. "He had a strange voice and got teased about that," she says. Happily, it was his voice that landed him jobs in TV and the movies.

Like her high school friend, Patricia also used humor to protect herself. "By the time I was in high school, I had learned to become the class clown," she says. "I was going to laugh at me before anyone else could. Talk about a standup routine—that was my life. I enjoyed it. I started to get a certain amount of acclaim, and kids really thought I was brilliant and funny. That was only the last year of my high school. Up until

Wise Words

" *When one is a writer, actor, dancer, musician of any kind, he or she does these things because they listen to that voice inside them. All of us have that voice.* "

then, I felt like one of the losers and geeks."

She's quick to remind kids of life after high school, and how things can change, especially for "late bloomers." She finds some justice in the fact that people like her friend have become very successful in their grownup lives. Patricia didn't start writing and illustrating her books until she was forty-one. Before that, she was busy raising her two children and did other work, including restoring art for museums. Patricia has an advanced degree in art history. She has also traveled extensively, including to Australia and Russia.

In the spring of 2001, she held a contest called "Stop the Teasing" to recognize schools that created a safe "tease-free" zone. She later painted a mural for the winning school in Virginia.

She also tackles teasing in the pages of her books. But not all her stories are about teasing. She writes about everyday events and extraordinary ones. Her first book, *Meteor!*, was about the big stir caused when a meteor came crashing to Earth, landing in her family's front yard. The whole town turned out to see it. Patricia's story shares the magic of the memory. Today the meteor is used as the family's headstone at a cemetery in Union City. Patricia also takes a small chunk from the meteor to schools and lets kids make wishes when they touch it.

Another new book is about a family reunion. *When Lightning Comes in a Jar* takes you to one of Patricia's family reunions, and she remembers how her grandma taught the kids to catch lightning in a jar outside the family farm.

Personal Stuff

Born: July 11, 1944, in Lansing, Michigan

Family: Patricia has two grown children, Traci and Steven, who live close by her in Michigan.

Favorite colors: Rich ones, with patterns on top of patterns

Favorite saying: "Of course it's a true story, but it may not have happened." That's what her grandmother, who was a fabulous storyteller, used to tell Patricia and her brother when they asked if one of her stories was true.

Favorite food: Pasta and all kinds of bread. Patricia loves to cook.

Favorite time of year: The winter holidays—from Hanukkah to Christmas. Patricia's mother was Jewish and her dad was Christian, so she grew up celebrating both holidays. She loves to decorate her home with five Christmas trees, including a book tree covered with mini-storybooks. Every year, she holds a holiday party for local children. Young guests visit, read holiday storybooks, and take home teddy bears or toys.

Today, Patricia lives in Union City. Her historic home is just minutes from the family farm where she grew up. Once a stagecoach stop, Patricia's home is now filled with treasures from her childhood, including her mother's and grandmother's dishes, rugs, and furniture. In almost all of the twenty-two rooms, you'll spot a couple of rocking chairs—because Patricia likes to do her thinking and writing while she rocks. When she's not writing, she's drawing or painting. She illustrates all her books with a unique and identifiable style. She mixes black and white charcoal drawings with bold, bright artwork. Patricia also uses photographs of friends and family mixed in with her amazing art.

Rock on, Patricia. We can't wait to see and read your next book!

Who's Your Favorite Author?

Brittany Levin
Age 8

My absolute favorite author is Patricia Polacco, without a doubt. I was lucky enough to have her visit my school for a half a day. I have many of her books, and I am one of her biggest fans. Patricia's stories are written about her family, friends and other people in her life. They are real, not make-believe. They are so very interesting. She even uses real photographs in the pages of her books.

One of my favorite books is called *Mrs. Mack.* In the story, Mrs. Mack loves horses and so do I. My mom even cried when I read the book to her. When Patricia came to my school, she signed all of my books. She also brought part of a meteorite that had landed in her front yard. I made a wish on it but I won't tell you what I wished for. Patricia Polacco is the coolest author in the world!

R. L. Stine

A Frightfully Good Writer

R. L. Stine writes so fast it's scary.

R. L., whose initials stand for Robert Lawrence, started writing funny little stories when he was in elementary school and never stopped. He just got faster and faster. In fact, he's written more than 275 books!

R. L. started writing books when he was a kid in Bexley, Ohio (near Columbus). He always loved scary stuff, especially scary comic books like *Tales From the Crypt*, and going to scary movies like *Creature from the Black Lagoon* and *The Fly*.

He also spent hours at an old typewriter (that was before home computers were invented), tapping out stories and joke books to hand out to friends at school. "I was always the class clown," he said. "Everyone thought I was very funny."

Everyone, that is, except his teachers. "I would take my books to school and pass them around, and teachers would take

them away. They told me—
even begged me—to stop
bringing them to school."

R. L. remembers making
hundreds of those little
books. He loved writing so
much that a brand new typewriter was what he wanted for
his present at his Bar
Mitzvah, an important celebration for thirteen-year-old
boys in the Jewish faith. He
got one and continued to
write.

But until high school,
none of his teachers recognized his talent. The high
school newspaper advisor was
different. She called R. L. in
and said, "You're so funny.
How would you like to write
a funny column for the newspaper?" She was the first
teacher "who was really nice
to me and encouraging."

After high school, R. L.
attended Ohio State
University, where he worked

Personal Stuff

Born: October 8, 1943, in Columbus, Ohio

Family: R. L. Stine lives in New York City with his wife, Jane, and dog, Nadine.

Special collections: "I have a pretty nice collection of eyeballs," says R. L. "Lots of fans give me eyeballs and other nice things." He uses them to decorate his home office.

Recommended reading: As a kid, R. L. loved reading science fic-tion, fantasy, and Greek myths. He also loved *Mad* magazine and *Tales From the Crypt* comics, which he had to read while getting his hair cut because he wasn't allowed to read them at home.

Free time: R.L. likes watching old movies, reading (especially mys-teries and thrillers), and taking Nadine for long walks.

Awards and honors: Stine is the #1 U.S. children's author in terms of sales. He's published more than 260 books, including over 150 scary stories. In 2000, R. L. received several awards, including Nickelodeon's Kids Choice Award. He's very proud of these awards and displays them in his office.

Wise Words

66 *A lot of kids who want to be writers worry about being published. I tell them, 'Don't ever even think about it!' I wasn't published until I was 28. Just keep writing and write for yourself. Writing is the one thing in life that I could do competently and well. It was the only thing that was ever easy for me. I never had any trouble writing. I've never had writer's block. I'm just lucky.* **99**

first as a writer, then editor of the student-run humor magazine, *Sundial*. Shortly after graduating, R. L. headed to New York City, where he hoped to write for magazines. He had a series of jobs, eventually landing at Scholastic, where he worked on children's magazines, including starting the humor magazine for teens called *Bananas*. A book editor thought R. L.'s writing was really funny and asked him if he wanted to write a children's book. That was the beginning of R. L.'s career as a children's book writer. His first book was called *How to Be Funny*. Many silly books followed. Eventually, R. L. began writing stories that were a bit frightening as well as funny.

In 1986, he penned his first scary novel for teenagers, *Blind Date*. Several novels followed before he launched his Fear Street series, the first scary-book series for teen readers. In 1992, he decided to create a line of scary (but funny) books for younger readers. Goosebumps, the most popular young reader series ever, was launched. R. L. thinks the stories are a lot like the scary (but goofy) movies he saw as a kid. From 1992 to 2000, he wrote *two books every month*—one for his Goosebumps series and one for Fear Street. "I don't know how I did that," he says with a laugh.

In 2000, R. L. launched another series, with weird and spooky story lines, called The Nightmare Room. Right now, he's writing just one book a month. "It's almost like being on vacation," he says, compared to the nightmarish schedule he kept for about eight years. R. L. is the top selling author for young readers, with more than 300 million books sold.

Where 2 Write

You can write to R. L. Stine at this address:

R. L. Stine
c/o HarperCollins Children's Books
1350 Avenue of the Americas
New York, NY 10019-4703

Check out **www.thenightmare room.com** for scary fun and for special online-only stories.

Coming up with so many good books and writing them is a bit scary for most of us to imagine.

How does he do it?

"It's not for humans," he says, laughing and showing us his crooked typing finger. He bangs out his books with just one finger—the result is a crooked finger. "I'll never learn how to type. It's too late now," says R. L. with a chuckle.

But there's nothing that unusual about how he works. He treats his writing just like any other job. Where does he go to work? He writes in an office in his apartment in New York City. The apartment has eleven rooms—which is huge for any apartment, but especially for New York City! He shares his office with his dog, Nadine, a King Charles spaniel. In the corner, he keeps the doggie crate where Nadine naps while he does his writing. Nadine even has Beanie Babies in her bed to sleep with. He writes early in the day, six days a week. When he's finished writing for the day, he likes to read, play pool, and take walks around New York City with his wife, Jane, and Nadine.

Where do all those creepy, funny, crazy ideas come from, anyway? Not from his walks. Some, he says, come from his own memories of being a kid. He remembers things that scared him—silly stuff like being afraid to park his bike in the dark garage. But most of his ideas start with nothing more than a title.

He spends a lot of his writing time just thinking up good titles. "I think of a good title and then I know it will lead me to a book," he says.

"Then I start thinking: 'Just where does that title lead you?'" After the title, R. L. thinks up an ending. Then he

AMAZING...

When he was a boy, R. L. loved Halloween. One year, he wanted to have the best costume. Something scary, like a skeleton. His parents went out shopping and picked out a costume for him. When they brought back the package, R. L. tore into it excitedly. "It was," he sighs, "a duck costume—a duck with a fuzzy tail! I was a duck for Halloween. It was horrible!" R. L. says his family didn't have much money when he was growing up, especially for extra things like costumes. So he had to dress up as a fuzzy duck for several years.

He later used that experience in his Goosebumps book, *The Haunted Mask*.

But True!

spends about three days writing a complete outline of the book. It usually takes him about two weeks to write the book from start to finish. Wow!

His life isn't all work. Just like your family, the Stines take vacations. R. L. and his family love going to Disney World. He and his son, Matt, have been more times than they can count. They also spend time at their summer home, away from New York City.

Is R. L. ever scared he'll run out of ideas for stories?

No. But he is scared of what might happen if he ever stopped writing. Before R. L. started writing scary stories, he used to have the same nightmare over and over. At least once a month he would dream there was something big and scary chasing him. He would always run through a series of rooms, slamming doors, trying to get away.

"It was really terrifying," he says. And then, "I started writing scary

Try This

Take a tip from R. L. Stine and start your writing with a title. R. L. starts every book by thinking up a title. For all the years he has been writing, he always starts that way. Spend some time thinking up a great title yourself, and then try to write a story based on it. Read TV guides, magazines, and even billboards for interesting words and phrases. R. L. Stine found the name for his *Goosebumps* series in the TV listings. His local TV station had an ad featuring a week of scary movies and called it "Goosebumps Week." The ad caught R. L.'s eye and he knew it would be his series title.

books. I never had the dream again. I always wonder if I stopped writing these books, would the dream come back?"

We don't want to know!

Book List

Fear Street series (June 1989 - June 1998), **Ghosts of Fear Street series** (July 1995 - October 1998), **Fear Street Sagas series** (March 1996 - November 1999), **Seniors Fear Street Super Chiller series** (July 1989 - July 1998) **Goosebumps series** (1992 - 1997), **Goosebumps 2000 series** (January 1998 - January 2000), **Give Yourself Goosebumps series** (July 1995 - February 2000), **The Nightmare Hour** (1999), **The Nightmare Room series** (September 2000 - ongoing), **The Haunting Hour: Chills in the Dead of Night** (2001)

Who's Your Favorite Author?

Rebecca Marshall
Age 13

I love reading and writing, especially scary stories. R. L. Stine is my favorite author. When I won lunch with him in a writing contest, it changed my life. I had written a scary story. When we got the call that I won, my mom started screaming and so did I. At the lunch, I talked to R. L. Stine and realized how big his passion for writing is. At the time, R. L. told me that he was writing two books a month. I wondered how that could be done and it finally clicked in my head that he can do that because he loves doing it. Writing is his passion. I learned that if you have a goal and set your mind to it, you could do it no matter what. R. L. Stine has changed my thoughts about books. The reason I love his writing style is because it is so real, yet so untrue all at the same time. His books take me out of the real world. He scares me with silly things. It is fun because it makes my imagination work, but I know it is not real.

Lois Lowry

Memories Make Moving Stories

*M*emories. Everybody has them. But for Lois Lowry, they become books. Lois has used her lifetime of memories to write more than thirty books, including her memoir (the story of her life) called *Looking Back: A Book of Memories*.

Lois, who was born in Hawaii, and grew up moving to many places around the world, has had lots of experiences and adventures. "My father was a dental surgeon in the U.S. Army," says Lois. "During World War II, he was on a hospital ship named HOPE, and later on an island called Tinian in the Pacific. At the end of the war, he went to Japan and became head of Dental Services at Tokyo General Hospital."

Through all her family travels, what Lois remembers most about growing up is how she felt about things.

For Lois, it was very hard making friends because her family moved so often. "A child's world consists of that small circle of friends," she says. She remembers being very shy and turning to books as her friends. Luckily, her house was full of them. "I lived in the world of my imagination," she says. "I always read a lot."

"Book characters are great company. Even knowing that they are fictional doesn't keep the reader from feeling them to be real and making friends of them."

Books can be great companions in happy and sad times. Lois remembers that as a child, she always wanted to have a close friend. But making friends took time, and friendships were sometimes interrupted by the many moves. She says she eventually found that one special friend—when she was fourteen. She still keeps in touch with that friend today.

What kind of company did Lois keep? Lois took comfort in her books. One favorite stands out—*The Yearling* by Marjorie Kinnan Rawlings. Lois also read all the Nancy Drew and Bobbsey Twins books.

AMAZING...

Lois is a gifted writer, but did you know she is also a great photographer? You can see one of her photographs on the cover of *The Giver*. "A magazine sent me to Cranberry Island, off the coast of Maine, to write about Carl Nelson [an artist] and to photograph him. I kept a copy of one of the photos I did, and years later used it as the book jacket for *The Giver*. He had a remarkable face," says Lois.

But True!

"In the 1940s, when my mother read *The Yearling* to me, that was when my awareness of world literature began. It's fair to mention that when my mother was reading, my father was over-seas in World War II. Mainly I can remember my mother begin-ning to cry about a part in the book. I realized her weeping wasn't just the book, but it trig-gered a whole flood of feelings."

Where 2 Write

You can write to Lois at this address:

Lois Lowry
c/o Houghton Mifflin
Company
222 Berkeley St.
Boston, MA 02116-3764

After hearing that story and seeing her mom's reaction, Lois knew that sad stories could be very moving.

Lois says her first stories were "wildly romantic, sentimen-tal, filled with improbable coincidences, overwritten, and prob-ably quite boring." But Lois adds that "writing badly is how you learn to write well. As a child I had many notebooks and I filled them with poems, beginnings of stories, lists and notes and observations. Jotting things down is certainly a good process for a writer." Lois says to remember that writing let-ters—or e-mail—is simply another way of doing that.

Lois thinks it's okay to write about sad events, as well as read about them. "It's important to tell our stories to one another—not just the cheerful and happy ones. All people, including children, have experienced anguish. It's very impor-tant to tell it and talk about it. Don't let it remain a great lump inside."

Lois traveled a lot and lived in many foreign countries as a child. Although most young people don't get to travel the world that way, Lois says that you don't have to travel to be a good writer.

"A child's world—including mine—consists of a small circle, maybe a neighborhood. It doesn't matter for a writer whether you're in a foreign country or your own backyard in Detroit or Atlanta or Houston. My memories are memories of friendships and families." Everybody has those.

Lois starts her book ideas by thinking of a character. "Once a character is firmly in my head, then I begin to fashion a story around them."

For example, in working on one of her Sam book series, Lois takes notes first on her computer screen about some of the characters' personalities. She'll write, "Becky: Crybaby" and "Emily: Gets Carsick." For Lois, those notes help

Try This

Lois Lowry uses her memory of growing up for lots of her stories. Lois's father was a good photographer so she has loads of family pictures.

To tap into your own memories, flip through a photo album or a box of photos. "Any photographs that trigger a strong feeling, you make those the beginnings of stories," says Lois. Maybe that special photo is from a family vacation or a picture of you and your best friend on the first day of school. Let that photo inspire a story, or try writing an essay about the memory inspired by that picture.

Personal Stuff

Born: March 27, 1937, in Honolulu, Hawaii

Family: Lois has four children and four grandchildren and lives in Cambridge, Massachusetts.

Free time: Lois likes photography, gardening, knitting, reading, and cooking.

Favorite books: Lois loves biographies now. Growing up, she loved to read books with girl characters, including the Nancy Drew mystery series.

Favorite food: Mexican

Awards and Honors: Lois has published about thirty books, including her popular and award-winning Anastasia Krupnik series. *The Giver* and *Number the Stars* both won Newbery Awards.

her map out the story. She knows who she is writing about. That's why her books are full of interesting characters.

The people—more than the settings or even the plot—interest Lois the most. Lois says her mind "is always crowded with characters."

Lois's first book for young readers, *A Summer to Die*, was published in 1977. In this book, she draws on her relationship with her older sister, Helen, who died of cancer at age 28. In the story, Meg and her popular and beautiful sister Molly are adjusting to their new, small home in the country, where they share a bedroom. Meg is resentful, more than ever because of her sister. But then her sister gets sick and Meg's world changes. Lois uses her memories of having a sister, and of her grief when her sister died, although the girls in the story are much younger than she and her sister were.

Two of Lois's books have won Newbery awards, *Number the Stars* and *The Giver*. The initial idea for *Number the Stars* came

Wise Words

> " *People interest me the most. I start with a character and once a character is firmly in my head, then I begin to fashion a story around him or her.* "

from a friend's true story of her life in Denmark during World War II. Lois used a combination of her imagination, her friend's story, and historical research to shape the story of friendship and of a young heroine in Denmark who helps her Jewish friends while the Germans are in charge of that country.

Lois's other Newbery winner, *The Giver*, is a complicated story that sets up a society that has no memory of the past, and a community that is supposed to be perfect. The story gives readers a lot to think about. Although the story is purely from Lois's imagination, the idea was born from her fascination with memories, and the question of what would happen if a whole group of people had no memories of the past.

"I find memories are often the beginning of stories," says Lois. Who knows, perhaps your memories could make good stories, too!

Book List

A Summer to Die (1977), **Find a Stranger, Say Goodbye** (1978), **Anastasia Krupnik** (1979), **Autumn Street** (1980), **Anastasia Again** (1981), **Number the Stars** (1989), **The Giver** (1993), **Looking Back: A Book of Memories** (1998), **Zooman Sam** (1999),Gathering Blue (2000)

Hannah Berman
Age 11

*M*y favorite author is Lois Lowry. Her book, *The Giver*, takes place in the future. It's about how it would be if the world was perfect. I really like the main character, Jonas. Jonas lives with his family in a community where there is no fear, color, or love. Jonas is assigned the job called Receiver of Memory. I would picture myself as Jonas. We are both smart, caring, and strong believers. I have read many books this year so far, but *The Giver* is way up there on my list of best books. I am really glad I read *The Giver* because now I know that a perfect world really wouldn't be perfect.

Andrew Clements

A Constant Reader and
A Clever Writer

*I*f you love the books of Andrew Clements, thank his parents, who taught him the importance of books and reading.

"I know the reason I became a reader. I grew up in a home where books were valued. Every Christmas, books were on the list," says Andrew, the author of many popular books, including *Frindle* and *The Landry News*. "We got all the other stuff, too, but I could count on a new book for every holiday. And I still have them all."

As a kid growing up in Cherry Hill, New Jersey, and later Springfield, Illinois, he never imagined he'd grow up to be a famous author. "The idea never crossed my mind," says Andrew. "I was a reader. I read *a lot*."

One of six children, Andrew loved to play outside with his brothers and sisters. In the summers, he would spend time with his family going to the lake, or playing games from sunup to

The secret ingredient to good writing is time. You will amaze your-self at what a good writer you are if you spend time on it.

sundown with lots of friends and relatives.

When the weather was bad and Andrew had to be indoors, he would read tons of adventure novels. "I remember reading all of the Hardy Boys mysteries, and graduating on to Sherlock Holmes. And I read all of the books by Jack London. I also liked true adventure stories, biographies and history," he says.

By the time Andrew started school, he was reading all the time. Andrew's favorite school subjects were English and read-ing. He had one special English teacher, Mrs. Bernice Rappell, who encouraged him by writing a note on a poetry assignment. The assignment was to write a mock epic poem—a funny poem in the same style as the older serious poems about heroes and their adventures.

She said his poem was really funny, so funny it should be published. "I got an 'A' on the assignment, which was unusual because she was a tough teacher," says Andrew. Earning that encouragement from such a challenging teacher really left an impression on Andrew. Her influence helped Andrew feel confi-dent about his writing, enough to make English his major at Northwestern University. He later dedicated a book to Mrs. Rappell, *Double Trouble in Walla Walla*.

After finishing his degree at Northwestern, Andrew signed up for a one-year master's degree program in elementary educa-tion. A year later, he landed a job teaching fourth grade. He spent the next seven years teaching—first he taught fourth grade, then eighth-grade English, and later high school English in the northern suburbs of Chicago.

After seven years of teaching, Andrew and his wife, Rebecca, wanted to pursue music as a career. His wife was a singer and very active in Chicago area theaters. Andrew played the guitar, and they had an act in mind. Andrew describes their act as "two voices and one guitar."

They sold their home and, with their two-year-old son in tow, headed to New York City to try their luck as performers. Though they had some success performing as a duo, they decided music wasn't the right fit for their family. Andrew got a job in book publishing, and they later moved to Boston, Massachusetts.

He also began writing his own stories. Andrew spent the next twelve years doing all kinds of writing jobs, from editing and translating to writing textbooks, and even several picture books.

Book List

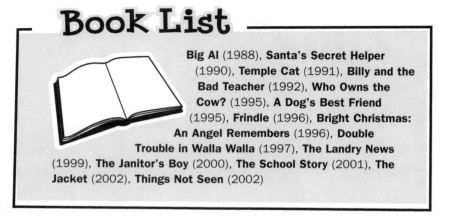

Big Al (1988), **Santa's Secret Helper** (1990), **Temple Cat** (1991), **Billy and the Bad Teacher** (1992), **Who Owns the Cow?** (1995), **A Dog's Best Friend** (1995), **Frindle** (1996), **Bright Christmas: An Angel Remembers** (1996), **Double Trouble in Walla Walla** (1997), **The Landry News** (1999), **The Janitor's Boy** (2000), **The School Story** (2001), **The Jacket** (2002), **Things Not Seen** (2002)

Personal Stuff

Born: May 29, 1949, in Camden, New Jersey.

Family: Andrew has two sisters and three brothers. He is married with four sons, including twins. His sons are in high school and college; although older, they have given their dad some friendly criticism on his books. Andrew lives in central Massachusetts.

Favorite books: As a boy, Andrew read the Hardy Boys series, Landmark biographies, Sherlock Holmes mysteries, and books by Jack London.

Favorite food: Fresh-baked bread, right out of the oven.

Free time: Andrew still loves playing outdoors and is a big fan of mountain biking, hiking, and canoeing. He also likes to draw and doodle, and plays the guitar.

Honors and awards: Andrew's most popular novel, *Frindle*, won the Christopher Award and many Children's Choice Awards.

Frindle, his first chapter book, was published in 1996 and was a turning point for Andrew. The success of *Frindle* made it possible for Andrew to focus on writing books full-time. *Frindle* is the story of Nick Allen, a fifth-grader with a reputation as a bit of a cutup. He loves to try to sidetrack teachers at the end of class to avoid homework assignments. His stalling tactics earn him an extra assignment on the origin of words. The assignment gives him a brilliant idea—to annoy his language arts teacher; so he makes up the word "frindle," as a new name for a pen.

Andrew actually came up with the word "frindle" when he was visiting a school in 1990. He was talking with students about the way words are invented by people's use of them. To illustrate the point, Andrew pulled a pen from his pocket and made up the funny word "frindle" on the spot, as a name for a pen. (You can read more about the story of how the book came to be at www.frindle.com.) Andrew later turned the story of that event into the award-winning book, *Frindle*.

Andrew has based some of the characters in his books on people he has known from his years as a teacher. For *The Landry News*, Andrew created Cara Landry from an event that happened in one of his classes. He remembers one first day of school when a student named Al Lande introduced himself as a journalist, and told Andrew that he published the *Lande News* every Friday. Al wanted to set up an interview with his new teacher, Andrew. He said, "You're the news this week." Andrew later used that experience as a beginning for his character, Cara

Try This

Details make the difference. Andrew says his favorite advice to offer students is to write about things that they know about. "Base your writing on experiences you've had, places you've been, things you've seen, and people you've met," says Andrew. If you want to create believable characters like Andrew's, it's so much easier if you base the characters on people you know. Then you also have your own experience to draw upon. "You can pull details from experiences you've had." Try creating a character based on someone you know. Write an opening page to a story that introduces the character. Make sure you have plenty of detail to bring the character to life.

Landry, a journalist who creates a student newspaper in *The Landry News*.

Although the story is completely made up, Andrew got what he calls "the first kernel" in that one event. Now, both *Frindle* and *The Landry News* are being developed as movies.

Andrew compares his job to running a small business. His day starts with helping his wife get the kids ready for school. "A typical school day includes getting the troops up and launched," says Andrew with a laugh. They have three teenage boys still at home and one at college. Then he begins his daily writing. When he's not writing, he has other book-related work to do, including answering e-mail, checking in with editors, and doing interviews.

Often, he'll visit schools to speak to students. As a former teacher, Andrew loves to talk with kids and teachers. He often gets ideas from visiting classrooms. Andrew keeps an idea file on his computer. "It's a long list of stories I've started to write, or ideas I might write about." Says Andrew, "When an idea goes running by, I usually try to catch it."

Keep catching those great book ideas, Andrew!

Where 2 Write

You can write to Andrew at this address:

**Andrew Clements
c/o Simon & Schuster
Children's Publishing
Division
1230 Avenue of the
Americas
New York, NY 10020**

You can read about Andrew online at: **www.frindle.com**

Hena Bhaya
Age 12

I love the book *The Landry News* by Andrew Clements. I especially like the character Cara Landry. In the book, Cara had just moved to Denton Elementary School. Her mom and dad just got divorced and she was getting over it. When she started school, she went to Mr. Larson's class. She never thought that in her new school, she would have somebody like Mr. Larson who would rather read his newspaper and sip his coffee than teach.

Cara loved writing so she decided to write *The Landry News*. She wrote the truth and believed it was right. She wrote that there was no teaching, but there was lots of learning in Mr. Larson's class. She dared to write the truth, and that is what impressed me about Cara Landry.

Margaret Peterson Haddix

A Farm Girl Grows Ideas

*W*hat if . . .

"It's probably safe to say that practically every one of my books started with a 'What if?' question," says Margaret Peterson Haddix.

In *Just Ella*, Margaret's question was, "What if Cinderella didn't have a fairy godmother, but figured out how to defy her stepmother and get to the ball on her own?" In *Running Out of Time*, the question was, "What if kids were growing up in a historic village, and their parents didn't tell them what year it really was?" In *Turnabout*, the question was, "What if scientists could make people un-age?"

Where does Margaret get such a fertile imagination that leads her to think of these interesting questions? It took root at an early age at her family's farm sixty miles south of Columbus, Ohio. "I liked making up stories," says Margaret. Ideas were always "bubbling up," she says.

Margaret was in many ways a typical farm girl. She was in 4-H for ten years, from grade school through high school. She raised and showed animals and took 4-H projects in sewing, cooking, genealogy, photography and—"not so surprisingly—in writing," says Margaret.

"In junior high and high school I also worked on my school newspaper and played flute in the band," says Margaret.

Margaret fondly remembers her years in the high school, which "was big enough to offer several different extracurricular activities, but was also small enough that students could try out several different skills instead of having to focus in just one area." She acted in school plays, sang in the chorus, ran track, and participated in an academic challenge team. Margaret did well in school, but that doesn't mean one of her favorite subjects, writing, came easy. Her frustration was that the ideas came so fast that she couldn't

Try This

Margaret gets some of her ideas from reading newspaper articles and magazine stories that interest her. She advises young writers to write about what interests them. Keep a file of clips from interesting stories in newspapers and magazines. When you're looking for inspiration, pull one out and ask Margaret's favorite question: What if? Margaret says she tells kids when she visits schools, "Write what you're interested in," just like you "read what you're interested in."

Personal Stuff

Born: April 9, 1964 in Washington Court House, Ohio

Family: Margaret was raised on a farm with two brothers and a sister. She still lives close to her family's home. Margaret is now married and has two children in elementary school.

Free time: Margaret helps volunteer at her children's school and in her community. She also loves to travel. Her family takes regular vacations. She likes being outdoors and really loved a recent trip to California's Yosemite National Park.

Favorite books: As a girl, Margaret liked books with girl characters, including all the classic stories. Another favorite was *The Mixed-Up Files of Mrs. Basil Frankweiler* by E. L. Konigsburg.

Awards: Margaret has received many state reading awards and American Library Association Top Ten Best Books for Young Adult honors, the International Reading Association's Children's Book Award, and American Bookseller Pick of the Lists.

keep up with them when she tried to write them down.

Margaret remembers, "I was a big bookworm as a kid, and I read constantly. I read a lot more than I wrote—I always had ideas that I wanted to write down, but the process was always painstaking, because my handwriting was so slow. My handwriting wasn't so good because my mind was racing to the end of the story."

Margaret says she did better once she learned how to type—and to type really fast.

"When I started working on computers once I was in college, I felt like I'd finally found a way to eliminate all the tedious parts of the process, since I didn't have to go back and retype everything whenever I wanted to make a change."

Luckily, she always had a lot of good teachers who encouraged her creative writing. She also had parents and grandparents who loved to read with her.

She went on to major in English at Miami University of Ohio, as well as history and journalism. After graduating, she had several jobs, including being a newspaper copy editor and, later, a reporter.

Says Margaret, "While I was working in journalism, I wrote several short stories and made several attempts at writing a novel, but never quite finished. I didn't start writing *Running Out of Time* until I'd left journalism."

She left her newspaper career when her husband took a job in Danville, Illinois (he was a fellow journalist).

In Danville, a small town, says Margaret, "there were very few job opportunities for me, so we decided that it was my chance to focus intensely on fiction. I took a series of part-time jobs doing freelance business writing and teaching at a community college, and used the rest of my 'workday' to write."

She finished both *Running Out of Time* and *Don't You Dare Read This, Mrs. Dunphrey*, within a year and a half. But then it took another year and a half before she managed to sell them.

Book List

Leaving Fishers (1997), **Among the Hidden** (1998), **Just Ella** (1999), **Turnabout** (2000), **The Girl with 500 Middle Names** (2001), **Among the Impostors** (2001), **Takeoffs and Landings** (2001), **Among the Betrayed** (2002), **Because of Anya** (2002)

"I had just turned thirty when I sold *Running Out of Time*, and was thirty-one when it actually came out," she says. Her second book came out the following year.

By then, Margaret was also busy raising two young children. She worked around her children's nap schedules at first, writing whenever she had a few quiet minutes. Finding time to write became easier when her children started school.

Where 2 Write

You can write to Margaret at this address:

**Margaret Haddix
Simon & Schuster Books
c/o Children's Publishing
Division
1230 Avenue of the Americas
New York, NY 10020**

"I have blinders on when I write," she says, laughing, meaning she can shut out everything else. Margaret admits that sometimes "an idea grabs me and I become obsessed by it."

Today, she writes mostly in the mornings after her children, Connor and Meredith, head off to school. She tries to work and write straight through lunch, then heads out for errands later in the afternoon.

Her children think of her mainly as a mom, not a famous writer, but her daughter has decided "she wants to be an author *and* an illustrator when she grows up," Margaret says. "My son is more blasé, but he thinks it's cool when his friends have read my books."

Margaret has written many books. Her most popular series,

Wise W🖊rds

" *Don't get discouraged if your story's not as good on paper as it is in your head. It's fine for your story not to be perfect the first time you write it out.* **"**

beginning with Among the Hidden, deals with questions of personal freedom. The series is set in the future and revolves around a government law that bans families from having a third child during a time of food and supply shortages. The ban continues, though, even when goods are plentiful in this pretend place.

The idea for that book originally started with a conversation about overpopulation with her husband, and decisions about having children. If you've read her books, you know how realistic this future world seems, and how you get caught up in the adventures of these hidden, or "third," children who are fighting for their freedom.

Margaret finds inspiration in many places. One place this former journalist finds ideas is in the pages of newspapers. Says Margaret, "I do actually keep a file of newspaper and magazine clippings that pique my interest, but I'm fairly lazy about using it. If an idea grabs me, I don't really have to go to the trouble of cutting anything out or filing it or taking notes. The best ideas usually hang around."

Margaret also finds ideas in her everyday life. As a busy author who frequently travels, the idea for *Takeoffs and Landings* came to her in an airport while waiting for her flight. She was on a promotional book tour and began to wonder: what if a mother had to travel a lot and needed to build a closer relationship with her children? In this book, the mom decides to take her children with her on a business trip to improve the family relationship.

This is one book in which Margaret uses some details from her growing-up years. For example, the two children live on a farm, just like Margaret did. The girl is active in 4-H, like Margaret was, and caught up in her small-town activities. Beyond that, of course, Margaret used her imagination to weave the stories of the widowed mom and her two kids.

Margaret always keeps some paper handy, never knowing when an idea might hit her. Then she writes her stories on a computer in her small home office.

When she's not typing her ideas at a fast-flying pace, she's always thinking. This former farm girl has a crop of books planned for the future.

AMAZING...

Margaret used to show hogs at the county fairs in Ohio when she was growing up.

But True!

Who's Your Favorite Author?

Sarah Maize
Age 13

I think Margaret Peterson Haddix is an excellent author and I like all of her books for many reasons. One reason I like her books is because can relate to them. She writes about characters with problems that I can relate to and I put myself in their shoes.

Another reason I like her books is because she mainly writes about my two favorite genres: realistic fiction and fantasy. She always finds an interesting way to tie them together so you get the best of both worlds in one book, which I think is really awesome. A third reason I like Mrs. Haddix's books is because she uses such great detail that you don't need pictures. To me, detail is important because it's what draws you in. If you can't visualize the book then it's a waste of time. I also like her books because they get you wondering what the world or your life would be like if her books were true. All of her books also have great morals that teach you valuable lessons. I've read and enjoyed every one of her books and I'm anxiously awaiting any new material.

Avi

Writing for Every Reader

***N**ot* many people can get by with just one name—but Avi can. His name is recognized by readers everywhere. He is the popular author of fifty books, including two Newbery Honor books, *The True Confessions of Charlotte Doyle* and *Nothing but the Truth.*

With so many books to his credit—with stories full of animal adventures, historical mysteries, tales of suspense, even sports stories—you'd probably think that Avi never struggled with writing. But that's not Avi's story. Writing doesn't always come easy—and it didn't for Avi.

Avi was born in New York City and raised in Brooklyn, one of the city's famous neighborhoods. Avi has a twin sister (today, she's a poet and a writer) and an older brother.

As a little boy, Avi loved books and being read to. His favorites included *The Pokey Little Puppy* and *Ferdinand the Bull.*

His home was full of books. His mom was a social worker and his dad was a psychiatrist, and their family loved reading.

"My family tells this story... that I came running down the steps of my home at the age of five, shouting, 'I can read. I can read,'" says Avi.

He says he wishes he could remember what he was reading that caused him such excitement. But what he does remember is that books were an important part of his life from an early age.

Avi says he was an early reader and enjoyed all kinds of stories—from comic books to history and science. "Every Friday afternoon, my mother would walk my twin sister and me and my older brother to the public library. Long before I had a Social Security number, a draft card, or driver's license, I had a library card. You could say it was my first identity card."

Every birthday, Avi received a book as a present. He still has some of those books today.

Although he loved learning, school was not always much fun for Avi. As a boy, he was shy and wasn't much of an athlete or a sports fan. He remembers liking science, but says he wasn't a very good student.

Where Write

You can write to Avi at this address:

Avi
c/o Harper Collins Children's
Books
1350 Avenue of the Americas
New York, NY 10019

You can also find more about Avi and a helpful list of his books, by subject category, on the web at:

www.avi-writer.com

Wise Words

"My twin sister—she was considered the bright one; my older brother, a genius . . . and there was me," says Avi.

Although he didn't know it at the time, Avi had a learning disability. Avi didn't learn that he had this disability until he was forty. It's called dysgraphia (dis-GRAF-ee-uh), and it means that his brain sometimes confuses words.

Avi still remembers, "I would write true sky, instead of blue sky." His brain would mix the words up. Even worse, his teachers had no idea why Avi was struggling. "They thought I was just sloppy," says Avi, and "not paying attention."

The idea of a learning disability never occurred to Avi. (Avi doesn't like to spend much time talking about it today. He says overcoming it "is nothing heroic.") He just thought he was a bad speller.

By high school, when Avi was still having trouble with reading and writing, he transferred to a school that focused on those subjects. He also got extra help from a family friend, a teacher, who tutored him.

His writing improved and so did his confidence.

"She changed my life," says Avi, about his tutor. "I was sixteen and gawky and shy. She told me, 'You're a very interesting person. If you wrote better, people would know that about you.'" Avi says her advice was just what he needed to get

Personal Stuff

Born: December 23, 1937, in New York City

Family: Avi has five children. Two are at home—in middle and high school—the other three are grown up. He and his wife, Linda, live in Denver, Colorado.

Favorite books: As a child, Avi liked adventure tales by writers such as Rudyard Kipling. He also loved comic books.

Free time: Avi likes to read and cook and go snowshoeing and cross-country skiing.

Honors and Awards: Library associations and a variety of educational associations have praised Avi's many books. He has two Newbery Honor books: *The True Confessions of Charlotte Doyle* and *Nothing but the Truth.*

motivated. He hadn't thought about writing in that way before.

Avi had another reason to write well. Her name was Alice. Avi wanted to wow her with his writing talents. Alice never was interested in him—or his writing—Avi remembers with a laugh.

Avi kept writing. He even submitted an idea for his class play, a tradition at his school. It was rejected in favor of another.

But that rejection didn't deter him. After graduating from college, where he studied drama, he started his writing life as a playwright. Plays seemed easier, Avi thought, because they depended on dialogue. "I thought it would be easy to pick up," he says. In his family, writing seemed like a natural career choice. After all, Avi is from a family of writers.

"Two of my great-grandfathers were writers. My maternal

grandmother was a writer, and my mother's sister was a writer, and two of my first cousins were writers. Both my parents wanted to be writers, although they opted in time for other professions."

It wasn't until after Avi married and started his own family that he began to write books for young readers. How did that happen? A friend asked him to illustrate a book and Avi said, "I'm a doodler, not an artist."

But the friend kept badgering him. Eventually, Avi gave the doodles to his friend for the book project.

The publisher liked Avi's doodles more than his friend's book. The publisher wanted to see more of Avi's art.

"I told them, 'I'm a writer not an artist.'"

The publisher came to agree and offered Avi the opportunity to write a book.

Book List

Things That Sometimes Happen (1970), Snail Tale (1972), No More Magic (1975), Captain Grey (1977), Emily Upham's Revenge (1978), Who Stole the Wizard of Oz? (1981), Bright Shadow (1985), Wolf Rider (1986), The Man Who Was Poe (1989), The True Confessions of Charlotte Doyle (1990), Who Was That Masked Man Anyway? (1992), Nothing but the Truth (1991), Poppy (1995), What Do Fish Have to Do with Anything? (1997), Poppy & Rye (1998), Perloo the Bold (1998), Ragweed (1999), Ereth's Birthday (2000), The Christmas Rat (2000), Don't You Know There's A War On? (2000), The Good Dog (2001), Crispin: The Cross of Lead (2002)

That led to Avi's first book, published in 1970, *Things that Sometimes Happen*. In the summer of 2002, Avi's fiftieth book, *Crispin: The Cross of Lead*, was published, along with a reissue of his first book.

Among those fifty books, there are stories for every reader. Avi has no trouble writing different kinds of books. He's written historical novels, thrillers, animal fantasies, and even ghost stories.

"I simply write the stories I wish to write, that have emotional meaning to me. I was never taught to write in any formal sense of the word; that is to say, I never really took literature classes beyond high school."

In college, Avi says, "I avoided English classes like the plague. I was entirely self-taught. Being self-taught, I was never pressured or pressed into one style, one format, or genre of my own. By the same token, I claimed all formats, all genres, and all styles as my own." Avi firmly believes that the way a story is told is as important as the story itself.

AMAZING...

So where did the name Avi come from? Although Avi is willing to share details about his life, he's not willing to use his given name. Avi is a nickname given to him by his twin sister when they were very young. Today, Avi is the only name he uses—and it's a name that millions of readers know and love.

But True!

Try This

If you want to be a writer, start with a short story. Don't expect to write a big fat novel right away. Try writing something smaller, just two or three pages, or even a short poem. Then after you've finished your work, try improving it. Rewrite, rewrite, and rewrite again, thinking up new ways to improve your story each time. By the fourth time, "you're seeing the story's potential and can make a real breakthrough," says Avi. Avi also says that writing poems is a good exercise for young readers.

Where does Avi get the ideas for his books? Young readers are always asking him that question when he visits schools. He gets ideas for his stories in many ways. His Dimwood Forest series, featuring Ragweed and Poppy, began when Avi found a book about a naturalist who rescued an owl. He thought he might write a story about the owl.

But when he set out to tell the story, something different happened. Other animal characters became the stars. A hedgehog called Ereth really wasn't going to be a big part. But readers loved the grouchy hedgehog, and eventually Avi created a book, *Ereth's Birthday,* with Ereth as the star.

"I never lack for ideas. To be sure, I don't use all these stories. Very few ever become a book. The stories that I choose to write or publish, the stories that I work on for a year or so that it takes to create and rewrite endlessly, are those which have particular meaning to me," says Avi.

Avi does most of his writing in an office in his home near Denver, Colorado, on a computer. He likes working on the computer because he constantly rewrites and revises his stories as he creates them. Avi says he has rewritten some stories as many as fifty times until he's satisfied.

And that's why readers hope Avi will write fifty more!

Who's Your Favorite Author?

Anna Spencer
Age 12

My favorite author is Avi because he wrote the first chapter book I ever read, and reading is now something I really enjoy. The first Avi book I read was *Poppy*, and it was very funny. I liked the talking animals especially. Whenever I'm not sure what to read, I'll choose an Avi book.

Avi writes a lot of books, so almost all of my friends like Avi too. I like Avi books because most of them are funny. They have many different parts, so there's always some action. I like fast moving fantasy and mystery books. Most books with sequels have cliffhanger endings, which are awful when you're really into the book. Avi's stories are enjoyable and fantastic. I hope many others enjoy his magnificent book creations.

Readers Have the Last Word

You've finished this book, but wait! We heard from many of you on your favorite writers. Here are some final words from kids who give their hot picks for great reading. Want to know what to read next? Just request a book these readers recommend—and don't forget to ask your own friends: "What are you reading?"

Taylor Rogers, age 11
Recommends books by Sharon Creech
Sharon Creech is my favorite author because her stories are very realistic. She has very detailed writing and makes it seem like you're actually there with the person. Her stories are in first-person so it is like someone you know very well, like a long-distance best friend, is telling you how they're spending their time. Most of her stories are about children that have had an outrageous experience. I really enjoy these books because she is so descriptive and she tells about things that could happen in real life to normal kids like me.

Sam Keeble, age 9
Recommends books by Matt Christopher
I like Matt Christopher books because they're cool. They are about mysteries and sports. Some of the books have a lesson to

be learned. One book I like is called
Snowboard Showdown. Two brothers go to
a snowboard competition, and Freddy,
the younger brother, wants to prove that
he is better at snow-boarding at any cost.
The books are incredibly good because
they have action, and I have learned more
about sports.

Matt Christopher books have inspired me to write my own
book. It is called *Home Run* and is about baseball, football, and
soccer. Matt, the main character, gets hurt in football and baseball so he tries soccer. It has some action and a little mystery.

Ryan Sila, age 10
Recommends books by C. S. Lewis

C. S. Lewis is one of my favorite
authors. He writes a very good series of
stories called the *Chronicles of Narnia.* I
love the way in some stories he has kids
go through an object, and enter the

world of Narnia, and then days later come out of Narnia, but
no time has passed. C. S. Lewis is definitely one of my favorite
authors. If you happen to come across one of his books, don't
just skip it, READ IT!

Paul Williams, age 14
Recommends books by J. R. R. Tolkien

There are four reasons J. R. R. Tolkien is my favorite

author. First of all, J. R. R. Tolkien writes classic stories, but they are very understandable, unlike most of those kinds of books. He also makes the story so vivid that the reader can picture every scene.

The second reason is that his books have all I want in a story. What I like is mystery, action, and horror. He combines all these ingredients to make a perfect modern classic, which allows it to be enjoyed by people of all ages.

The third reason I love his books is that he makes the story seem and feel vivid, real, and very possible even though it is fiction. When he describes the characters, Tolkien uses the detail to make the book even more entertaining than television or Nintendo.

My final reason is that his books opened a whole new side of reading to me which I had never known about before. He made ordinary fiction books seem extraordinary. He made the science fiction books that I had always thought were nerdy and geeky seem interesting and enjoyable.

Mariel Richter, age 12

Recommends books by Valerie Tripp

Valerie Tripp is my favorite author because she writes about American girls from different time periods who have taken a stand in what they believe in. Valerie Tripp [author of many of the American Girl series books by Pleasant

Company] has also inspired me with her writing to do things I

never would have done, such as writing my own stories and poems. Reading about the character of Kit Kittridge has also made me want to help people out.

Kalyn Saulsberry, age 9

Recommends books by Ann M. Martin

Ann M. Martin is my favorite author. She has inspired me to start writing my own stories. I have already started writing a book about a famous tennis player. Ann M. Martin has written some of my favorite books, including *Snail Mail No More* and *The Doll People*.

Snail Mail No More is a great book because some of it reminds me of what happened to me. My best friend left the school. It made me sad, but it also helped me make new friends. This year I'm getting more friends. In *Snail Mail No More*, Elizabeth's best friend Tara moved out of the state. Elizabeth and Tara made new friends, but then they were a little jealous of each other. *Snail Mail No More* has taught me not to be jealous of my friends when they make new friends. Ann M. Martin wrote this book with her friend, author Paula Danziger. Ann M. Martin's stories have inspired me to be a writer when I grow up. Her books are the best!

Megan DeMarco, age 12

Recommends Anne of Green Gables by L. M. Montgomery

The author that inspires me most is L. M. Montgomery. She

wrote the Anne of Green Gables books. Last school year, I read six out of the eight "Anne" books from December to May. She changed my view on books. I usually read mystery books, but when my librarian suggested *Anne of Green Gables*, I decided to read it until I got another book. I started reading *Anne of Green Gables* and it was great. It made me want to read all the time.

Last summer, I went to Prince Edward Island and looked at all the Anne of Green Gables attractions. I tasted raspberry cordial like in the book. I visited Green Gables and the Haunted Wood. It all seemed so real.

Diana Ivezaj, age 13
Recommends books by Roald Dahl

My favorite author has written some wonderful books. His words seem to pop off the page and capture my imagination. His stories take me to different worlds, each one more strange and crazy than the last. Sometimes I laugh, sometimes I cry, but either way, I always want to pick up the book and read it again and again.

His name is Roald Dahl. I have read many of his books and enjoyed all of them. Roald Dahl's unique style of writing is what makes his stories so fun to read. His words flow together like music, and the characters make the stories so interesting.

The first Roald Dahl book I ever read was *Matilda*. Another one of my favorites is called *The Twits*. One of the reasons I enjoy Dahl's books so much is his zany characters and their hilarious actions.

There are many surprises and unexpected endings in his books that make the stories fascinating and funny at the same time. Roald Dahl really makes me enjoy reading. Once I pick up one of his books, I never want to put it back down.

Brice Jurban, age 12

Recommends books by H. G. Wells
The Invisible Man, The Time Machine, The War of the Worlds, perhaps you've read these books. They were all published by one man, Herbert George Wells. H. G. Wells is possibly one of the greatest fiction writers. H. G. Wells's stories really

get me tingling in suspense when the story unravels all at once.

My favorite book I've read of his is *The Time Machine*. It's so cool how he describes the future with the Morlocks, and how he interacts with his characters.

I recommended everyone to read H. G. Wells's books—they're something you can't pass up. I guarantee you'll read them over and over again since they're so good!

Michael Hyman, age 10

*Recommends **Poppy and Rye** by Avi*
Poppy and Rye is about a mouse named Poppy who is going to marry another mouse named Ragweed. This is the sequel to the first book, *Poppy*. Poppy is my favorite character because she is so

courageous and doesn't give up. Poppy is a strong, tough mouse that has a lot of curiosity that takes her a lot of places.

Jae Kim, age 13

Recommends **Perloo the Bold** *by Avi*

Avi is a person that gives writers and bookworms something more than books. He gives pieces of work. His books— which come in all shapes, categories, and titles—are made for people when they are young or when they are bent with age. I am one of those bookworms. I discovered Avi at my old school, which had a huge library. It was there that I began my interest in Avi. The first book I read of Avi's was *Perloo the Bold*. This story was extremely adventurous and a page-turner. It was the first book that made me really think about what might happen in the next chapter.

Matthew Wrobel, Age 12

Recommends R. L. Stine's books

I love horror stories; they're my favorite type of books. His books make me feel like I am right there at that very moment!

Marilyn Reid, age 11

*Recommends **Anastasia Ask Your Analyst** by Lois Lowry*

I love Lois Lowry because she is the author behind the Anastasia books. My favorite book is *Anastasia Ask Your Analyst*. It was detailed and very funny. Anastasia is the funniest girl. She is very sophisticated and smart. She has a whole series of books written about her. I have read all of her books except *Anastasia at Your Service*, which I plan to read soon. I'd recommend these books to girls of all ages.

Calling All Readers

Want to see your name and opinion in print like these readers? Beyond Words Publishing publishes many books that include opinions from young readers. Check out their web site, **www.beyondword.com**, for the latest contests and new books.

Who knows? You could find yourself in the next book!

About This Book's Authors

Janis Campbell and Cathy Collison have been writing partners and friends for years. They have collaborated on two books for children and a curriculum guide for teachers. They write and edit together at "Yak's Corner," a magazine and a syndicated newspaper feature for young readers, based at the Detroit Free Press in Detroit, Michigan. They are both married with two children each. When they're not busy yakking, you can usually find them reading a good book.